zuckerbook

Jerry Zucker Middle School of Science
The Zuckerbook Project

Spring 2016

faculty advisor, CEO
Mr. Erik J. Hilden

internal production
Alex Pretto editor
Kenya Williams art director

art department
Jalen Corbin team leader
David Cattles marketing
Jan Patterson marketing
Cordell Johnson marketing

public relations
Jasmain Jenkins public relations lead
Samiyah Frasier facebook
Syncere Washington webmaster
Angela Scott twitter, swing position

accounting, management
Alfredo Flores chief financial officer, pinterest

cover art
Angela Scott

Published by **The Zuckerbook Project**, 2016, North Charleston, SC.

All rights reserved. Reproduction in any form, be it written, hand-written, paw-written (in case your cat or dog can write), photocopied, photographed, posted, or in any other form without regard to what that form might be, is strictly prohibited without expressed written permission (likely handwritten) from The Zuckerbook Project's Faculty Advisor.

Besides, it's naughty. Very naughty, indeed...

Copyright 2016 by **The Zuckerbook Project** in concert with:

The Students of Jerry Zucker Middle School of Science
6401 Dorchester Road, North Charleston, South Carolina 29418
Principal: Jacob Perlmutter

ISBN #: 978-0-692-69684-2

Printed in the United States of America.

Dedication

This work is dedicated to the students who created each piece that is contained within these pages. Their words, their art, their spirits, and their energies bring this work to life. May their voices always be heard.

Community Involvement

Endeavors such as these are evidence of the great things that can happen when a community pulls together in the face of adversity and produces a testament to the voices of their children. Without the support of our community, this would not have been possible, and without further support, future endeavors may not come to pass. We have had a lot of support this year, but we can always use more, as is true of any non-profit activity. If you are interested in donating to The Zuckerbook Project or are interested in volunteering to help in any way, please feel free to get in touch. I can be reached at erik_hilden@charleston.k12.sc.us or at the following address:

The Zuckerbook Project c/o
Jerry Zucker Middle School of Science
6401 Dorchester Rd. Room 159
North Charleston, SC 29418
843-767-8383 ext. 25614

Acknowledgements

Nothing makes acknowledging colleaugres and supporters easy. There's no way to do it. There are so many folks who have had a hand in this issue, I am not sure where to start. I could go with the cliche'...those who submitted work, who directed their students to be involved, who threw money at us, who did whatever, but that wouldn't be genuine. The people who really contributed to this publication, now in its fourth volume, are the people who made it happen. Some of them are teachers who directed students to bring us their work; some are people who forked over cash to support our publication; some of them are people who brought us new connections that are going to allow us to expand beyond our wonderful school and bring other schools into the fray. Each of them deserves gratitude, smiles, and a whole pile of thank yous. This is a short list of follks who were involved. My apologies to anyone who was accidentally skipped.

Mr. Jacob Perlmutter, our esteemed principal, has given us unwaivering support in the midst of his busy schedule, and allowing us to slim down the class that produces this work has made all of the difference. We will always be grateful for his support, and appreciate his allowing us the autonomy necessary to make this work. Without him, we would not be here, and you would not be reading these words. There is no measure to how appreciative we are, and shall remain. Bless Mr. Perlmutter, and thank you for allowing me to teach the Science of Publishing and Writing instead of Anthropology.

Ms. Erika Gilly has brought us new opportunities and connections to new schools that also want to publish the works of their students, and we are grateful to have the opportunity to do so. The Zuckerbook project has always wanted to spread its wings beyond the hallowed grounds of Zucker Middle School and bring new school into our group. She is affording us this chance, and we are grateful for the opportunity to bring new communities into the wonderful world of publishing. It is an important next step for The Zuckerbook Project.

Ms. Nikki Mustipher, Ms. Kelly Macomber, Ms. Angela Taylor, Ms. Elizabeth Gleim, and **Ms. Shorace Guider** continue to provide connections to students that I could never acquire on my own, bring writing to us that we are all to happy to publish, and support us in the other wings of the school. **Ms. Zan Gregory** continues to give us access to student artwork, which is the perfect compliment to student writing and a much appreciated contribution. This issue, we have more art than we know what to do with, and that is great. **The entire faculty and staff of Zucker Middle School** has continued to tolerate our pleas for donations, financial support, and our fundraising activities, and the janitorial staff continues to clean up after us without complaint. We are fortunate, indeed, and could not ask for a more supportive community at this school. Thank you. You are appreciated more than you will ever know.

Dr. Clark G. Hilden, who has continued to donate to our cause, deserves special mention, for donating large amounts of money and inspiration, support for our students, and mentoring as we go forward in the unchartered waters of small batch publishing. Take a look at his textbook, Uniquely Oregon, if you want an interesting read about a fascinating state created by a dedicated teacher of geography. It is fun to read regardless of your interests, and available at Amazon.com.

Cynthia A. Hilden also deserves special mention for her large cash donations and ongoing moral support, as well as her mentoring and dedication to teaching writing and reading. She remains an inspiration and a much appreciated supporter of The Zuckerbook Project, and for this we are grateful. Major kudos are necessary. Thank you.

Ms. Sarah Douglas remains, and always shall remain, a spirit guide on our journey. Her enthusiasm for our students and their work has always been remarkable, and the students that she now teaches remain among the most fortunate on the planet. It is my sincere hope that they know what a treasure they have on their hands, and I am proud to call myself her friend and colleague. Bless her and the work that she does.
She is a jewel in the crown of education, and teaching.

Mr. James Brooks helped me whittle down the class size for this school year, has been gracious in his support of what we are doing, and continues to bring us new and talented people, all of whom have contributed, in their own way, to The Zuckerbook Project and the products that we create. We thank him for being here with us, and for having our backs as we go forward with expanding the reach of The Zuckerbook Project. Mr. Brooks is an important ally, and for that, we are grateful.
This is by far the most cdreative group we have ever had, and Mr. Brooks is, in large part, responsible for bringing together these brilliant minds.

The 2015-2016 Zuckerbook Project Staff deserves a special mention here. Their contributions have expanded our reach from an erstwhile press release to a full on assault on social media, product development in our art department, and a focused editing department. Big things are on the horizon for us, and these fine young people have helped to make it happen. They have also helped me as a teacher, in showing me what is really imprtant in conducting this class, and what they need to learn, and it has been an invaluable learning experience as a result. Thanks, kids, you have humbled me once again.

To each of you, thank you. This book is as much for you as the students and communty with which we work, and we remain grateful for your involvement.

To the good people everywhere who have decided that Zuckerbook is worthy of support, thank you for purchasing our books and thank you for believing in our fledgling project. Without you, the energy to continue might not exist. We are grateful for your support, for you are the people who will spread the word, and will bring us into the front lines of young adult literature. Thank you so much for your support. You are forged in gold.

The Mission of The Zuckerbook Project is, and shall remain, to produce the very highest quality Student Publication of Literary Works intermingled with Visual Art, while Remaining Faithful to the Zucker Middle School Student Experience, and then distribute it to the community, so that our voices may be heard. Let them always be heard.

Open it and read…

-- Mr. Erik J. Hilden, March 31st, 2016

zuckerbook

Contents

1. I Am............................ p1
2. The Joys Of Camping......... p15
3. Coming Of Age p25
4. On The Holocaust p33
5. Insights p49
6. On Nature.................... p63
7. On Change p81
8. All About Love p87
9. Troubles And Struggles p105
10. Politics, As Usual p123
11. From The Mouths Of Babes... p129
12. Really Short Stories p147
13. The Dark Side p159
14. A Short Story.................... p171

Belen Martinez

1 I Am

I am Thoughtful

Miqueas Mendez

I am a student that is thoughtful.
I wonder when I will stop being a student.
I hear teachers teaching.
I see teachers writing.

I want to graduate from college.
I am a student that is thoughtful.
I pretend to be out of school by graduating.
I feel myself getting smarter.

I touch my paper and anything for school.
I worry people will try to hold me back.
I cry when I get bad grades.
I am a student that is thoughtful.

I understand that I could graduate from college.
I say I can pass my grades.
I dream of me getting a job after graduating.
I try to do my best in everything.

I hope to not let people hold me back.
I am a student that is thoughtful.

Oscar Hernandez

I am Aristic and Intelligent

Mebron Cayasyab

I am artistic and intelligent.
I wonder about what it is like outside in the universe.
I hear the most majestic beast I can imagine.
I see anything that my imagination takes me.
I want to make a new step for mankind.

I am artistic and intelligent.
I pretend I am epic.
I feel majestic things in my dreams.
I touch anything I can imagine.
I worry the obstacle ahead of me.
I cry at the story of Benjamin Button.

I am artistic and intelligent.
I understand I will be made fun of because of my race.
I say there's hope no matter how you're feeling.
I dream about my imaginations.
I try to do my best in art.
I hope my dreams come true.
I am artistic and intelligent.

I am Caring and Brave

Cassie Drollinger

I am caring and brave.
I wonder what I'll be like when I'm older.
I hear the birds singing.
I see myself getting older.
I want a good future.

I am caring and brave.
I pretend to fly.
I feel different.
I touch my dog.
I worry about my family and future.
I cry because I don't like change.

I am caring and brave.
I understand that life isn't perfect, that it's hard.
I say that it will get better.
I dream about summer days.
I try my best in everything I do.
I hope for my future.

I am caring and brave

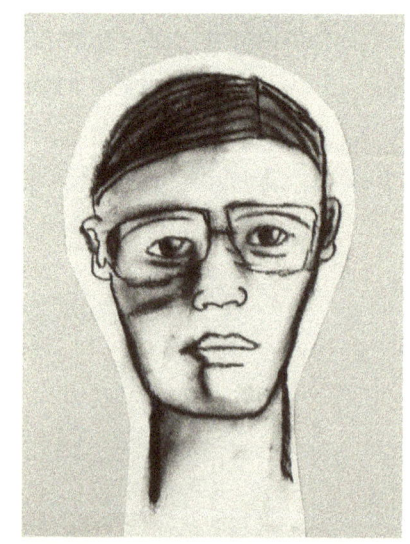

I am Focused and Sharp
Cierra Goodwin

I am focused and sharp.
I wonder what my life will be like when I grow up.
I hear the wind blowing back and forth.
I see the sun when I wake up, and I see the blue sky.
I want to be great and successful.

I am focused and sharp.
I pretend to be shy and funny.
I feel nervous and funny.
I touch the shutter knobs.
I worry about my mom and dad.
I cry when something is wrong and I get a failing grade.

I am focused and sharp.
I understand my work at home and school.
I say let's be happy forever.
I dream about what my life is going to be like when I grow up.
I try to understand things in life.
I hope it happens someday or sometime today or anyday.

I am focused and sharp.

I am Fun and Silly

Neil Ventura-Victoria

I am fun and silly.
I say I will be successful.
I wonder if my older sister is sad.
I dream I'm the older brother.
I hear a car going really fast.
I try to be as good as my older sister.
I see things that are happy.
I hope I'm a good brother.
I want to be smart.

I am fun and silly.
I pretend that I am the older brother.
I feel bad when my older sister is alone.
I touch a light that gives me energy.
I worry I'm not a good brother.
I cry when ever my little sister sleep.

I am fun and silly.
I understand I'm the only brother.

I am Kind and Smart

Shamyu

I am kind and smart.
I wonder how cases are made.
I hear the bees talking.
I see colors whenever I spin around.
I want a colorful pony.

I am kind and smart.
I pretend to be asleep.
I feel water when it's not on a flower.
I touch the 3D screen in the movie theater.
I wonder when I study too hard I may forget.
I cry when my family members die.

I am kind and smart.
I understand the way of life.
I say anything is possible if you put your mind to it.
I dream I will become a nurse.
I try to get all A's on my test.
I hope that I grow up to be responsible.

I am kind and smart.

I am Smart and Creative

Aliyah Chavis

I am smart and creative.
I wonder if I will pass all my grades.
I hear music.
I see me getting all "A's."
I want to go to college.

I am smart and creative.
I pretend that I am famous.
I feel proud.

I touch a microphone.
I worry that I will fail.
I am smart and creative.
I understand you have to do good in school.
I say I believe.
I dream that I am a singer.
I try to make good grades.
I hope to be famous.

I am smart and creative

I am Sharp and Cool

Semai Jamison

I am sharp and cool.
I wonder if i am good enough to do things.
I hear beeps in my head,
I see a short mile.
I want to be a scientist/ballet dancer.

I am sharp and cool.
I pretend to be a cat sometimes.
I feel happy and strong.
I touch victory before,
I worry if I don't pass,
I cry about my family death.

I am sharp and cool.
I understand people agree with others.
I say we need to be brave and fight for what we believe in.
I dream to sing one day.
I try to stay focused.
I hope to pass.

I am sharp and cool.

I am Smart and Beautiful

Vernasia Washington-Coardes

I am smart and beautiful.
I wonder if the ground is really hard.
I hear birds singing a song.
I see the trees are really big.
I want to be the president of the U.S.A.

I am smart and beautiful.
I pretend to sing.
I feel like flying in the clouds.
I touch the clouds.
I worry about homeless people.
I cry when I need my aunt but she's not here.

I am smart and beautiful.
I understand that school is important.
I say I need education.
I dream of going to the white house .
I try to trust people.
I hope I will be successful.

I am smart and beautiful

I am Smart and Kind

Bianca Cedillo

I am smart and kind.
I wonder what others think of me.
I hear my family laughing happily.
I see me and a kind dog by my side.
I want to be a veterinarian.

I am smart and kind.
I pretend to be happy all the time
I feel nervous around others.
I touch a dog.
I worry I will make someone else cry.

I am smart and kind.
I understand things can be frustrating.
I say math can be hard sometimes.
I dream of scary things.
I try to not get mad or frustrated.
I hope to progress in things.

I am smart and kind.

I am Sad and Angry

Quentin Xavier Writght

I am sad and angry.
I wonder if people laugh at me.
I see people talking about me.
I hear people laughing at me.
I want a brother or sister.

I am sad and angry.
I pretend to be calm when I'm angry.
I feel angry and sad.
I touch my heart.
I worry about dying or getting hurt badly.
I cry when I'm angry.

I am sad and angry.
I understand games can be educational.
I say tech helps me calm down.
I dream that I will have peace instead of nightmares.
I try to complete school.
I hope I can change and fix my issues.

I am sad and angry.

Monday, 8-24-15
Simone Capers

I am from

I am from a place
Where there's hatred and pain
I'm from a place with a lotta killing
And Guns so loud you can hear it through the cieling.

I am from a place where them nine people got shot
Every shot dropped a heart
With pain and tear drops
Why would be shoot at a holy church
Do they know what that's worth
they put alot of hurt,
Out in the world
Killing such innocents girls.

I am from a place where people think they tough
they act real buff
they be thuggin on the streets
But they ain't bettea then doggy meat

Bruhh guess wah thoe
I from South Carolin, Charleston

2 The Joys Of Camping

Camp Time

Kyla Wright

Camp time.
Birds singing their songs
As the sky hums.
Trees sway side to side,
As the water drips,
Leaves breaks into pieces,
When the animals scurry through,
As they're looking for food,
Staying quiet to take a bite.
Kids laughing with delight
While others frown.
Why be sad?
When there is much to explore.
Night time.
Spookiness surrounds you.
Dark sounds and objects…
All there is, is you and your food.

Camping

Kenny Coronel

Girls screaming.
Isn't that lovely?
Darkness arises.
Isn't that lovely?

Raccoons Terrorizing.
Isn't that lovely?
Boys put into a police car.
Well, isn't that just lovely?

Cold night.
That's just great.
Wind blowing.
That's just great.

Things being stolen.
That's just great.
Phones dying.
That was just great.

Gnats attacking.
I'm totally enjoying this.
Wooden Beds.
I'm totally enjoying this.

Cold water.
I'm totally enjoying this.
Clogged Toilets.
I'm really just enjoying this.

The food.
It was the best.
The memories.
They are the best.

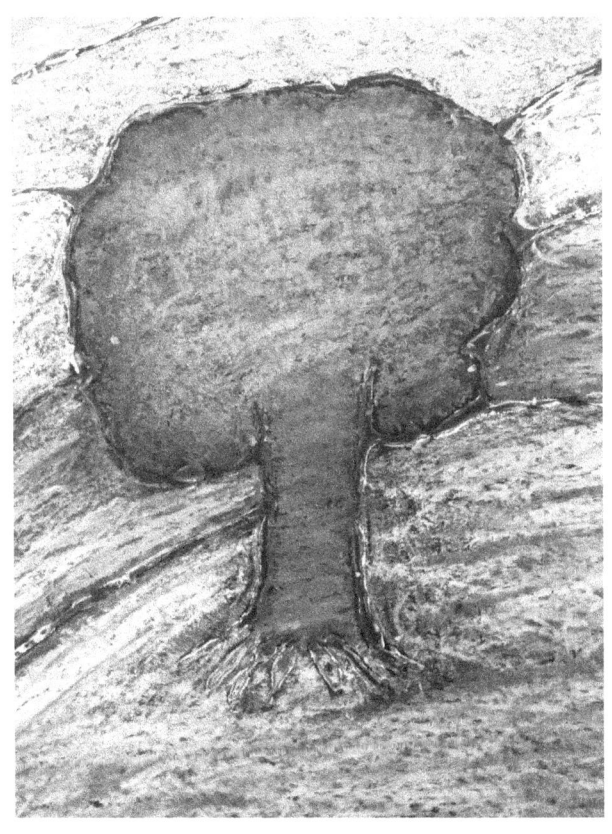

Camping

Kory Singleton

I woke up at 5...
Or rather, was forced awake.
Too many people in our tent,
And they forced a shake.

They all slept kindly,
Under the blanket of the night.
False warnings of rain
Had once filled us with fright.

Yet, I was the only one awake
To witness the moon
Shine brightly at 5.
The swaying water played a tune.

No one would witness.
They were all lazy bums.
They refused to get out of bed.
It all seemed a little dumb.

Why wouldn't they want to witness
Beauty in its truest form?
The nature of it all
Made one's heart warm.

The river was a leader.
You had to follow him.
You had to jump in,
Even if you didn't know how to swim.

Could You Move Over Please?

Jemiell Laguitao

A tent for four,
Yet we held more.
We actually held five,
That was, until two more came to our hive.

Cramped, it seemed.
Move over! one screamed.
I believe someone had sneezed.
Someone would say "Could you move over, please?"

Our tent, the loudest to be,
Joked and fiddled all night with glee,
Until someone went to bed, and all would freeze.
Someone would say "Could you move over please?"

Tight it was, in the night,
Conquering each others body with might,
Until finally someone let out with a wheeze.
Someone would say, "Could you move over please?"

Calm and collected, every one was,
As if presents were being brought to us by good ole Santa Claus,
Until the wind picked up, and woke everyone with a breeze.
Someone would say, "Could you move over please?"

Soon, someone let out.
Got up at 5 AM, and hissed with a pout.
He looked over all of us and finally said, "Geez,
Could you move over please?"

Murder at Camp

Alfredo Flores

I snuck out my tent last night,
For everyone was starting to fight.
"Let's play Uno."
"Let's play cards."

Sick of it all,
I went to take a sip
Of the water fountain
Down the road.

A quick moving object
Passes from behind.
Yes, I saw it.
I'm not blind.

I turn to see,
What could it be?
I move the thorns,
And I know what I saw, I sworn.

Addi Maples was dead.
She hung from the tall pine trees.
I couldn't believe what I had seen.
The culprit was gone & so was I.

No Sleep?
Devonte Alston

"We're not going to sleep at all!" Said Godwins and I. Until the boring activities and the bonfire, which lead me to stay in my tent for an hour.

Watched some dudes play basketball practically being a commentator against the subject when you come late.

Later at night twelve guys decided to sneak to the girls side and failed inevitably. A cop was present.

"Zzzzzzzzz"

Where did you come from?
Quinton Adams

"Where did you come from?" a cop with a bright light said to me.

I said nothing, tired pain in my heart. I was wearing all black and was as black as can be. I snuck in through the back way, sat down as if nothing happened, and with my friends, I chilled.

Even in the midst of the night, you blended in, or at least we thought.

We went in groups and wandered off in the place. We were very sneaky, but most of us were still caught.

Nothing was promised. Our desire was strong, but we still weren't safe.

It wasn't a good decision. I didn't really know if we should.

But it was all a second experience, and we were still camping in the woods.

Waves
Kory Singleton

We talked about people.
We talked about fame.
We talked about Eagles.
We talked about flames.

So many things were mentioned,
as we lay in the tent,
But things we didn't mention
Stayed inside out of fear of repent.

Everything else flowed easily,
Like water in the near-by stream.
Out words were the high-tide,
And in the water, they gleamed.

But we didn't know about the waves
That were to follow.
They rushed through in tons.
People running from cops, and running from guns.

Oh, the stupidity.
The people flocked in waves.
So many were caught.
So many water drops unsaved.

It's sad, really, though,
That on that night, it didn't rain.
Maybe the waves of people
Wouldn't have gone insane.

Storms may have arisen.
Bolts quicker than Usain.
Humans are 60 percent water,
And waves run through our veins.

Julia Guo

3 Coming Of Age

Masked

Katelynn Mansfield

The light is often masked
By the darkness.
Hidden from the eyes,
So often in plain site.

Light, the hope always in disguise.
Waiting to be revealed,
To be unmasked,
To shine though the dark.

All you need to do
Is know where to look.
To know that there is always
A spark of hope
In the darkness.

Growing Up

Kenny Coronel

When you were young,
Life was fun.
There were no such thing as tears,
Or things called fears.

You were curious.
Never getting furious.
You were so little.
Not knowing life would be brittle.

Now as you get old,
You ignore what's told.
You just cry
While everyone passes by.

You only have a couple of friends.
That's alright, it isn't the end.
It's okay you're getting older.
Your heart just gets a little colder.

You start losing feelings,
Without no meaning.
Who knows why?
You just lie.

You realize everything.
The real thing.

Not the false claims,
Because nothing was the same.

It's called growing up.

We'll Never Know

Ca'Shun Barr

I'm honestly not ready for high school.
It means I have to grow up...
Mature...
Childish, maybe, but my childhood is over.

I want to sit down,
Take a look around,
Just take in the beauty,
But there's never any time for that.

I guess I'm stuck in a constant loop of
Books, books, books.
Doomed to study forever.
But the MD is too important...
The degree we so desperately need.

Late nights, I guess, are worth it.
Results that aren't exactly promised, but oh well.
Does it all matter?
We'll never know.

What A Mystery

Jesus Verdugo

The future...what a mystery...
The learning, the teaching,
What awaits on time,
In high school.

What a work.
What they expect from me, everything on time.
My work, harder and harder.
But it all pays off, in time.

My graduation, will I be ready on time?
Then, to college...
Maybe to MUSC.
If you want to be a doctor, be on time.

What awaits of time?
Maybe my prompt...
My graduation...
The future...what a mystery.

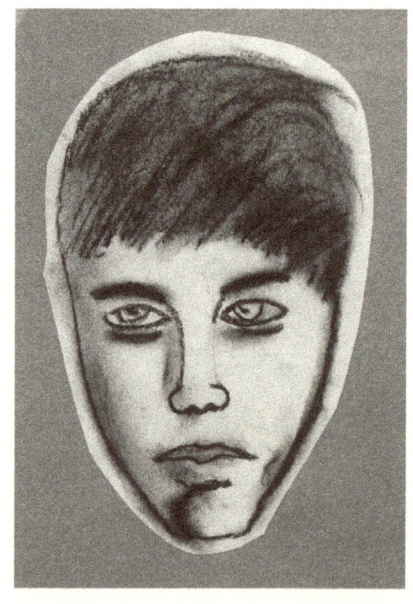

But, Beyond What I Can Feel

Jasmain Jenkins

One day, everything will go away...
All the pain.
All the shame.
And all the lies shared.

All the unforgettable cries and miserable nights
Of how you weren't there.

One day, I will stand up and say...
I MADE IT! I AM STILL STANDING, STRONG AND TALL!
WITH NOTHING TO MAKE ME STUMBLE AND FALL!
There is no shame in my game.
There is no crying coming my way.

I'm not
Changing my mind!
I will NEVER look behind for the future is beyond…
Beyond what I I can't see.
Beyond what I can't hear.
Beyond what I can't touch.
And...
Beyond what I can feel...

Because, deep down, I know it's there.
This is my dream...
To be free from all my iniquity.

If I Could Look Into The Future

Katelynn Mansfield

If I could look into the future, it would be to high school.

I am planning on going to West Ashley High. I've heard its a very good school, and it's often overlooked.

I just hope I get accepted into the school. I don't have everything planned out.

I guess you could say I'm taking life one step at a time. Some students say I should plan ahead, especially for college.

But what's the rush? Why should I worry about college when high school hasn't even started yet?

One thing I want is to live, not just survive. Too often, they are people that are very successful but unhappy, and others who give up and work just to get by. I find it ironic that we are told at a very young age that we can be whatever we want.

They make it sound so easy, no? That whatever we want to do will happen with a simple snap of your fingers? To be honest, I couldn't care less how much money I will make. Doing something that makes me happy is what I about care about the most.

May not have my life planned out, as one would think, however, I have a few Ideas on what to do…studying animal behavior and maybe even become a writer. I will also consider doing something history-related, but I am not entirely sure what.

Life doesn't always turn out the way you would like, and that's not a bad thing. My plans may change over time, it all depends on what God wants me to do with my life. I am putting my trust in Him for what ever he has planned for me in the future.

Only he knows what my life will be like ten years from now.

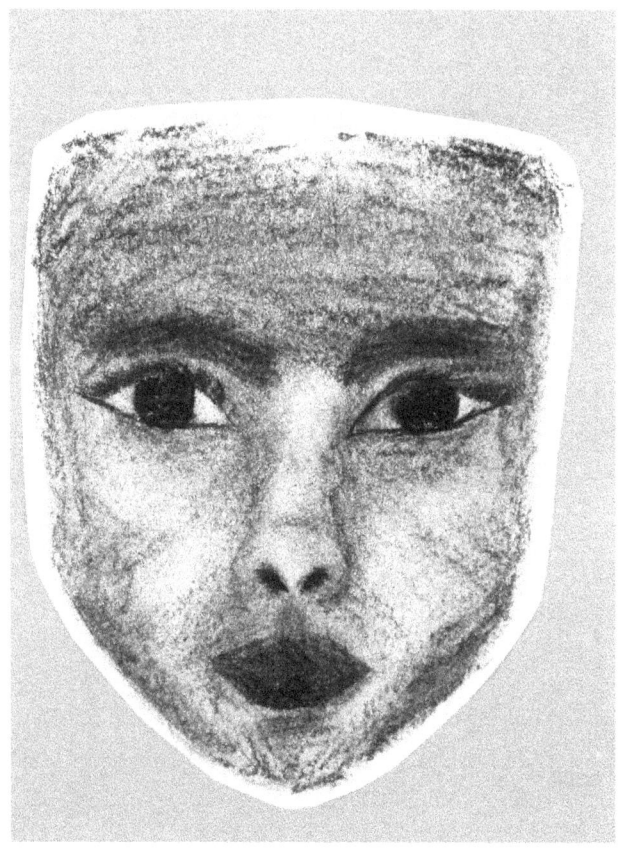

Belena Martinez

4 On The Holocaust

A Jew's Thoughts

Jessica Bevins

I live the life of a Jew every day.
Not knowing why I get discriminated against.
The concentration camp wasn't a good place to be.
Just working and wondering why they wanted me.

I struggled every day to support my family.
Having very limited access to things we need.
I have no freedom, no where to go,
Being pushed around everyday for so long.

I see my people dying every day.
Young children and the elderly with no work ability.
Wishing I could save those people from the hurt.
Knowing that if I try I'll lose my life.

As I know that Hitler and the Nazis want us gone,
We continue to work humbly and hard,
Wishing that we could have a change
Even though we know we cant have our way.

A Nazi Soldier's Inner Monologue

Kory Singleton

As I stroll through Auschwitz,
Head high with PRIDE,
I look over and see Jews,
Tears in their eyes.
To think they'd expected a good surprise,
but I still feel bad
to cause demise.
Adolf told us this thing would
all work out.
But up until the invasion,
He wouldn't tell.
Tell us what it's about.
He asked us to listen and comply.
We did,
but we can't do this, guys.

Look around,
See all the pain on the ground?
There's dead bodies.

We treat'em like dogs in a pound.
But… One man can't rebel.
I'll surely be treated
just like them,
Thrown in a cell.
I'll be starved to death,
and I don't really want to die tonight.
I have to go home to my kids and wife.

But wait...
Could it be the exact same way for them?
They're bigger men.
 bigger than we are.
They don't fight
for themselves.
I don't want to start apocalypse
because of this dictatorship.
Where are the U.S. BATTLESHIPS?
We can't let this happen again.
We can't forget the scars that
this has brung.
Or else, when we do
you'll hear the war bells ring.

Now this is just a prediction,
but there may be, nuclear weapons, or,
country to country alliances,
But Germany can't afford to lose.
We don't have the force to win.
Flee to China,

and hope they

get struck by Cupid.

Or else go through the open door policy.

Oh, can it be?

That my mind has changed on me!

That I fought for Adolf,

But I now know that we are weak.

It's unbelievable

That this is a REALITY.

I look over and see Jews,

Tears in their eyes.

To think they expected a good surprise.

But I still feel bad

To cause demise.

Adolf told us this thing would

All work out,

But up until the invasion,

He wouldn't tell,

Tell us what it's about.

He asked us to listen and comply.

We did,

But we can't do this, guys.

Look around,

See all the pain on the ground.

There're dead bodies.

We treat'em like dogs in the pound.

But... One man can't rebel.

I'll surely be treated

Just like them.
Thrown in a cell,
And be starved to death.
I don't really want to die tonight.

Disgust

Keyonne Mcknight

They sneer,
They scoff,
They glare,
They mock.

With no sense of humanity.
No dignity.
No Sympathy,
And no remorse.

They disgust me.
I disgust them.
They don't think I have the right to judge.
I don't think they have the right to judge.

Just a never ending cycle of hate.
A cycle of disgust over how cruel we could be.
I don't see a point in living,
Because all I see, feel, and live,
is disgust.

Don't Leave Us For Nothing
David Cano

The Holocaust,
A truly dark place,
Where Jews were rated the worst of the worst.
But before that dark time we were children,
We played, we laughed and loved our lives!
We were just defenseless, and innocent children.
We had a bright future.
We were going to be leaders, bankers, teachers, or anything
That would improve our lives,
We were gonna be special people,
With beautiful dreams that anyone could wish for.

But then...
They were gone in a blink of an eye!
I can remember screams in my grave still today!
At that time, us Jews were taken to the worst place we
Could've ever imagined,
The Holocaust, not a place in the world but that's what we
called it,
We were there to be separated from the world to be nothing!
We heard screams, cries.
We saw starving people, deaths!
Just because we were Jews,
With no one to speak out for us.
Remember us, the people whose dreams and lives
Were stolen away.
The Holocaust's dream...to kill us all,

Wishing us away with death's recipe, was successful.
Just don't stand in our graves and cry,
Because we did not die.
Our beautiful dreams are still alive.

I Live

Zamani Lyde

I cry, I hurt.
I feel, I hurt.
I know, I hurt.
I bleed, I hurt.

I cry for freedom.
I feel the pain.
I know the present.
I bleed for the future.

I know freedom exists.
I know pain hurts.
I know the present is dark.
I know there will be a future.

I cry, I live.
I feel, I live.
I know, I live.
I bleed, I live.

Humming That Little Song

Tekaysha Hagler

"Mom," said Jonny, "someones at the door for you."

"Who is at the door?" asked mom.

"A big and scary looking soldier with a big gun and a funny looking symbol on his uniform," said Jonny.

"Oh no..." she thought. "Baby boy, I want you to hide in that secret place your father has build for us in case of an emergency, and don't come out till I come and get you. OK?" Said mom.

"But mom, aren't you supposed to come, too?" Jonny said confused.

"Yes, but this is important," she said. "Don't come out of there if you hear any sound, like screaming. If you do, cover your ears and hum the song I sung to you every night before you got to sleep, OK baby?" she said crying.

"Yes, mommy," he said as he wiped her tears away with his tiny little hands.

As he did that, there was banging on the door and she said "Go now!" And he did.

Jonny rushed to the secret place as fast as his little feet could carry him, until he heard glass breaking, his mother screaming and crying, gun shots then silence.

All while it was happenings, Jonny was humming his little heart out quietly while covering his ears.

He heard loud foot steps and an unfamiliar language being spoken. He stop his humming, uncovered his ears and listened to the sounds of the foot steps as they came closer and closer to where he was, then walked away and continued there unfamiliar language talk that Jonny never understood. He waited and waited and waited for his mother to come get him, like she said she would, but she never came, and he kept his word.

More Different Than Needed

Keyonne McKnight

I have brown eyes,
I'm supposed to have blue eyes.
I like my brown eyes.
They hate it!

I have brown hair,
I need to have blonde hair.
I like blonde hair, but it's not me
They despise me now!

I'm too different.
I should be the same.
A pure being with blonde hair and blue eyes,
I taint the earth.

Now I need to be exterminated.
I'm too different.
The scum of the earth, that's what I am,
I'm too different than what is needed.

My Cries For Help

Jessica Bevins

HELP!!!!
Why do they not hear me?
Screaming in pain with barely a voice to scream.
Do they even hear me, or are they ignoring me?

Knowing that they dont care about me.
Saying that I'm an animal and inhuman.
Working all day to do the same working tomorrow.
Wishing that my aching body could rest.

HELP!!!
My second cry of help.
No one hearing me as lay on the ground.
Trying to get up but my body is too weak.

My fellow Jews come to my rescue.
My brotherly Jews coming to help.
When no one else was around to hear my cries.
Why must they work us so hard for their enjoyment?

Praying that my life is not over.
Living with diseases and open cut wounds.
Getting weaker, day by day.
I pray that I will live to see the day when we will be free.

Rusting The Iron

Yael Perez

Rusting the iron.
Dusting the floors.
Everywhere in here.
Ironing the clothes,
Surely some work
To be done neatly.
There wouldn't be a stop
To the deed, no drinking beer,
Soon arrives the train, soon
We walk and take our seat.

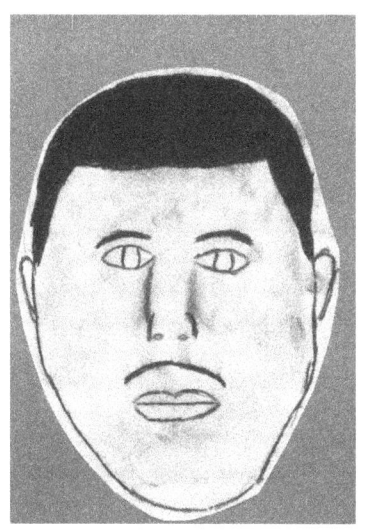

People and people, walking in stripes,
However, what is this, yelling and slapping with a rod?
Oh, it's a Nazi, yelling and knocking out the lights
Of some people, because some are just some sad sods.

There is many, maybe some, soon children start disappearing.
I wonder, I wonder, when I'll go,
Because once I knew the children were dead,
I started steering.
I wanted to yell, wanted to rebel, but I knew to stay low.

By the time it was the end, I knew what was next.
By that time, we entered, slothered and smothered together,
By the showers, by what I knew, I knew I was vexed.
By this time the showers sprayed, leaving the world, forever.

What, Who, Where Is Freedom...

Godwins Tuyishime

What, who, where is freedom?
I was born into this hell.
My pap and mammy talk
About freedom.
What is this thing?
What does it mean?

Today marks my 14th birthday>
The day mercy abandoned me.
But what is it?
What do I long for?

So what if my nose is bigger than yours,
So what if I have curly hair,
So what if I'm circumcised,
So what if my hair is not blonde...

Don't I deserve this thing called freedom?
Before mammy and pap left to work,
They told me of freedom.
I won't stop till my race can feel freedom...

Why Us?

Torrance Perry

Why us?
Why us?
Why do we have to go through such a terrible time?
Why are we hated because of our race?
Why are we forced to leave our homes?

What did we do?
Is there anything we can do to fix this?
Mother, when will we go home?
Father, when will we go home?

Will we ever eat regular food again?
Why do we all sleep together?
We wonder if there's a way for us to escape…
We wonder if the Nazis feel if there's anything
They did wrong…

Will we ever get out of here?
Father, why are all of my friends gone?
When will we be free?
Isn't this illegal?

We don't want to be here.
Why us?
Why us?

Survival

Keyonne McKnight

I need to breathe.
I need to eat.
I need to drink.
I need to live.

I'll do what I need to do to survive.
I disappoint myself.
I push, I hit, and fight to get a crumb of bread.
I block out all emotions to prevail.

I have no time to live.
Living are for those who can laugh freely.
Smile freely.
And love freely.

I must be vicious.
I must be prepare to slaughter.
Just to see the next day until it's all over.
Just to survive for I can live.

5 Insights

Achromatic

Keyonne McKnight

I am sorry for the way I behave.
I just need to see you.
To survive in this cold, unsightly world,
I need to sin to live.

I regret nothing even as I give these sincere apologies.
I need to breathe another day.
I put everything on the line just to win for you.
I would never want you to see me in such a devilish way,
but I need to protect you.

I need to see you again before all the chaos erupts.
Breathing like it's my last,
How to move,

How to feel,
How to see the world, I forgot long ago.

Everything is black and white.
I can't comprehend these thoughts,
Every details moves to fast before my unfeeling eyes.
Then everything,
Once so bleak, burst into a symphony of colors.
Oh, so beautiful.
It was all over before I realized I blinked.

The wind carries my melancholy goodbye.
I'm not quite ready to say goodbye, but I will try.
The past lies in what we were yesterday.
Tomorrow is what I will be.

I am ready to stand on my own and become me.
Not just surviving, but living,
No matter how many times these words
Spill out of my mouth, like the waterfall.
My eyes will still conquer.

Fair as the day, cold as the night.
Me and you will never collide,
As the moon and stars will never touch.
As close as they are, as perfect as they match,
It is never…
Never…
Going to happen.

Cameron

Everett Smith

Cameron is the name of a brave one.
The one that stands out, yeah,
The one that gets the job done.
The one that you know you can
Always look up to.
Yes, the one that always
Aims for something new.

Cameron, the name of a boy that's cool.
I'm talking cooler than wintertime,
Jumping in a pool.
If you ever try him,
You'll surely be a fool.
He always keeps a notebook.
Like a second tool.

Always consider others.

Life is not always about you.

James Aiken

Respect

Shorace Guider

Like, they want it...
But they have no idea what it is.
Their lack of knowing can be heard
In every curse word
They utter in your presence.

Through every sucked tooth and rolled eye,
That not getting it is really not told why.
You just felt belittled by some little old guy,
Who looked you in your eye and told a bold lie!
"You don't love us!"

The words cut deeper than you thought they should,
While you contemplated doing more harm than good.
Showing him that you could actually hack it in his hood,
Only wishing that sucka really would…

James Aiken

So then you could really show him what it is,
And in turn show them what it is.
That it's earned and not for free,
That it's learned and not from me.
That it begins with their family, their history…

Like I said, they want it, but they have no idea what it is.
It's just a concept; a word,
That keeps bouncing off their ears.
From lips, they've been taught, don't actually exist.
The same lips that tell them how it really is.
The same lips that they will actually never really hear,
Until…
Until it becomes too late,
And they are no longer here, because of their hate.
Because they only knew,
To imitate,
And never fully understood,
how to dictate,
This thing they say they,
"Want",
But, they have no idea what it is.
… It's respect.

And until they know, they'll never know.

Another Dream

Jemiell Laguitao

I once had a dream, at an age so young.
I rode what was in the deep sea, but flew in the air.
She was neither a dragon, nor a fish, nor a bird.
Yet it swam in midair, over and through the puffy white clouds.
She was a shade of deep blue, which almost blended perfectly
With the sky.

She breathed not through its mouth, but on the top of his head.
She had no teeth, nor did it smile, nor frown.
She was a tremendously enormous colossus which was
Frightening,
Both from up close and from afar.
Though it expressed no gestures, it's eyes,
The size of two baseballs,
Were elegant, gentle and calm.

She not only swam, but I also discovered that she sang.
She sang of words I did not understand, but with her flock,
They each sang a verse at a time gracefully
Though I did not understand her beautiful voice,
She spoke to me through my mind and thoughts.
At the end of our journey and her song, she would say to me,
"Wake up"
At that moment my eyes closed; opened to a shining light
From my window
I sat and stared out at the sky, for I was back in reality.
Feeling older as time flies by, I wait for yet another dream.

Drums

Angela Scott

As I began to play the drums,
The sound vibrates throughout my body.
I fall in love with the feeling.
I fall in love with the sound.

As I start to play softly,
I grip to the sticks with kindness.
I love the beat it makes.
I love the rhythm we make.

But then I drop the sticks.
They slipped through so easily.
I wish I could have known
That it wasn't that easy.

So now I sit with my sticks around me,
No beat to move my heart.
I fell in love with that sound,
But all I hear now is nothing.

Feelings

Yahira Gonzales

What exactly are they?
Why do we have them?
It seems feelings just get in the way.

Feelings stop us.
We tend to do things with our heart instead our brains.
Why do we do that?
It makes life harder than it is.

Without feelings, life wouldn't be right.
They make us who we are.
Even though they bring us down,
At times they make life worth living.

James Aiken

Good art
Devonte Alston

I met a guy named Finn.
He had black tops on his face.
They reminded me of the volcanoes.
He was rather an odd fellow.
He liked to put together puzzle pieces.
But he also liked to shape these weird creatures.
Being as odd as he was,
He was an artist who created this special kind of art.
Most of his sculptures had tails.
Some of them had sleek cuts on their faces.
Unlike me, some of those paintings lived in water.
They were quite amusing to me.
Aside from the pieces,
Some of his paintings lived where I did.
Much like me, they had four legs.
These Sculptures were in fact just like me.
Usually, a man's art could come from his character overall.
However, his personality was like sandpaper.
He was the solution to every rough patch.
This may correlate to his art.
But could I be just like him?
Maybe.
It seems pretty complicated to construct an archive of work.
Most importantly, am I capable of creating Godart?

I Don't Care
Syncere Washington

So what, you can't physically see my collarbone?
My thunder thighs have power.

So what, I can pinch more than an inch?
My chin has friends.

You try to downgrade me.
Try to belittle me.
Call me fat.

I don't care.

Okay, when I lift up my shirt, you can't see my ribcage.
My stretch marks make me beautiful.
I'm not afraid to show my rolls.

I like to eat
And I feel no shame in saying it out loud.
So what?
I don't fit society's vision of a perfect woman.

Who cares?
I certainly don't.

Save me

Keyonne McKnight

I bled out all my blood.
I cried out all my tears.
I screamed out all my fears.
I prayed out all my tears.

I don't know what to do.
There are no voices directing me.
Just deadly silence that constantly rings out.
The world now is in black and white.

My people die by the hundreds
From Hell's fire,
From poisonous acid showers,
From choking constricting air.

I need someone to save me.
I need to pray to god.
Or maybe I need to **sell my soul**,
I just need saving, **please**.

Wisdom

Alfredo Flores

You see that old man sitting?
Surely, he is wise.
For he is old,
And soon to die.

You approach him,
Take slow steps up his rotting porch.
He scowls at you for "invading his property."
Weren't you trying to ask for his advice?

Wisdom doesn't come with age,
It comes with how open-minded you are.
How wise are you when you
Can't accept someone for their beliefs?
How wise are you when you
Can't accept someone for who they are as a person?

Open your mind and you'll open the knowledge
That you want to spread across the world.
What's happening?
Why do you feel so inspired and free?
It's wisdom, welcome to your wise mindset.

Why should you value this?
It's what makes you different from the others.
You know what they wish they knew.
The word wisdom may be succinct,
But it's meaning is beyond value.

James Aiken

Morgan Zipprich

6 On Nature

Spring

Ca'Shun Barr

Spring is coming.
I feel it in the air.
The slight warmness and sense of birth,
A few animals coming out of hibernation.

The snow melting, and the grass coming to sight.
Flowers coming out of this beautiful yet dark Earth.
Though the light is soon to come,
When it does, let us all awake and rejoice,

Only for the fulfillment of birth and not death,
As the cycle continues, let life defeat death,
As light tries to fight darkness.

Sail Away, Winter
Alfredo Flores

Lavender strokes the sky at sunrise.
I went to the beach last night.
Not in body,
But in spirit.

I went to the beach to say my farewells
To my sailor, Winter,
For his boat left far away this morning.
But he will return at the death of Fall.

Slept in with Winter,
Woke up at the first moments of Spring.
The beach wasn't cold any longer,
It was fresh and alive.

The winds brought
Spring with his vibes.
The world woke up from its Winter's rest.
The dark toned colors in my skin turned into light pastels.

Closed my eyes at the near end of my time with Winter,
Only to open them with the pollen touching my eyes.
I was in my warm bed of darkness,
Now I'm in a bed of flowers next to Spring.

Winter was problematic,
Spring was bright and loved me.
Spring was gone,
But he's back for me.

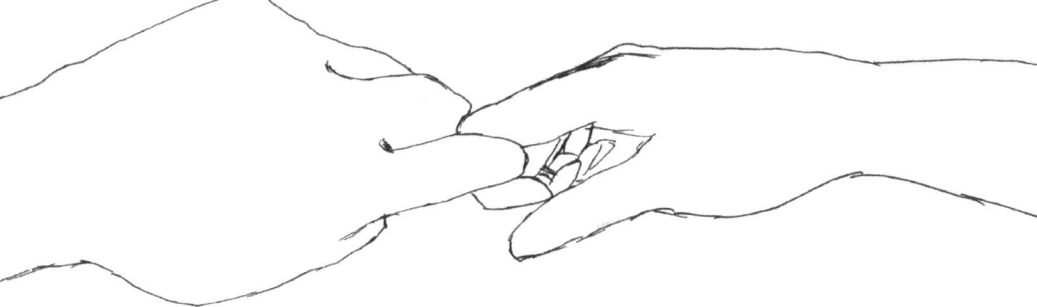

Angela Scott

Sunny Shine

Cameron Steinbacher

The Sunny shine helps us live.
We all stay happy as it rises.
We can all work together as it rises in harmony.
All it takes is for us not to be greedy,
But for us to be nice.
Once we elude ourselves of the false perception,
Before us, we will be fine.
For the Sun shall shine again.

That Lizard
Angela Scott

When I was younger,
I loved to play outside.
The blinding sun in my eyes,
The cool grass beneath my feet.

But then I came across a Lizard.
It looked friendly and beautiful,
But then it bit me and I started to cry.
In the end, I forgave that Lizard.

But here I am now.
I still love to go outside.
The cooling night breeze brushes past me.
The dark filled night sky comforts me.

But then, I came across that same Lizard,
Continuing to look friendly and beautiful.
But before it could bite me, I crushed it.
There was no crying,
No pain,

No hurt in the end.

Summer

Nadya Murray

Hot, thick air,
Little bits of cold breezes in the air.
Barely any movement of the people near.
The swarm of the mosquitos buzzing into your ear.
They dig in your skin without a care.
The sound of the cold treats are near.
The sound they say Happy Birthday
On this day of the year.
The best season.
Summer is here!

Kenny Coronel

Dark as Night

Cameron Steinbacher

As the Moon rises on the Eastern shore,
When the wolf howls in hunger and pain,
We all realize it's time to lock our doors,
For the evil of the night has come to visit.

The evilness to come to us is soft-spoken.
It finds us while we sleep, where we think we are safe.
It infects us to be greedy, and mad,
For nothing is safe from this ancient being.

As the townspeople flood the streets with rage,
The thieves get greedier and steal more than they need.
There is no light to this night in the town.
For it is as dark as night.

Life

Tyrell Alston

I finally feel the light on my face,
While sprouting I've reached the surface.
I'm ready to make my mark on the world,
I'm ready to have a purpose.

I'm free to do what I need to do,
which is to go and produce.
I have to go and develop O2,
for the people to put to use.

I'm starting to feel sick.
My leaves are falling off.
I can't really stop it.
I have a serious case of Fall.

I don't do much anymore,
I am done,
my time is now over.
Until I take yet another
Trip around The Sun.

Mother Earth

Jemiell Laguitao

Our mother,
She makes life appear to be a fantasy,
When in truth, life is merely just a reality.
She's bright, she's beautiful,
She's part of our beloved dreams,
Yet within brightness, there's darkness.
She's a marvelous nightmare that screams.

Our mother,
Her eyes, they shine and guide us
All through the night.
Her hair, so smooth and silky,
Like water that flows ever gently.
Her ears, through trees or plants
Or a conch shell, she listens.
Her lips, they softly kiss our small tender feet
For every step we gain.

Our mother,
She calls breezily,
Through the air of the wind that blows.
She whispers faintly,
And through the echoes of nature's journey,
She hums gracefully,
Through the birds and the trees that chime.
She sings gorgeously with harmony,
Through the soul of her great big heart.

Just imagine, you begin to taste salt water
Being sprinkled into your mouth.
You begin to smell dried seaweed
And salt misting the air.
You begin to hear the wind
Howling and the waves
Splashing gently and ferociously.
You begin to feel the sun's sensations
Beaming down onto your skin,
Just as well as the silken sand
Trickling between your toes.
You then begin to see those magnificent blue skies
Start to fade,
And the horizon appears
Right over the distant blue oceans.

Our mother.
Beautiful isn't she?
She just sits there on her throne
Spinning around elegantly.
She's a perfect paradise,
A heaven revealed under
The puffy white clouds.

Our mother,
She takes care of us,
She provides for us,
She loves us.
Yet we treat her harshly
Without any thought, sense, or care.

We throw trash directly
At her angelic face.
We pollute and intoxicate
Her fresh open air.
We cut down uncontrollably
At all of her creations
And beauty.

Our mother,
Though we treat her grimly.
She forgives
Without regret or question.
But why do this
To our beautiful pulchritudinous mother?
Our beloved Mother Earth.

Ghost Rider

Alyssa Kapinos

Why do I hear the sound of a galloping horse?
But yet I do not see one.
Why do I feel the spirit of one,
rather than see one with my own eyes?

I feel the wind that moves the lazy grass,
Rocking it back and forth.
The euphony of the horse's breath
And their graceful speed.

Why do I feel warmth when I am in this pasture?
Why can't I ride this horse, this spirit?
Why?
Why aren't I the ghost rider?

The Sun rises and the Sun sets.
Yet I still feel the horse grazing and munching
The luscious grass.
Day and night,
Still waiting for an answer to my questions.

I no longer feel the heart pumping.
I no longer see the rise and fall of my diaphragm.
I no longer see my reflection in the mirror.
I have finally become the ghost rider.

Future

Jan Patterson

The smoke is clouding, the Earth is shattering.
The life is evaporating, the cold is gathering.
Is life falling?
The animals are calling; they plead.
The water is turning into stone.
Volcanoes are erupting.
The stone is melting.

Earth is gone.
Is there a new planet in town?
The colors are red and white.
It is at the same place as Earth.
All the green and blue is gone.
Nothing has survived.

The plants, our life, and the air is gone.
Also the tiniest of all cells are gone.
The trees, leaves, and grass extinct.
The best of the world is vanished.
The air is poisoned from pollution.
Fires, pollution, global warming, we were the start of this.

The world has vanished.
From the people that destroyed the sky.
So the heat ball of fire can hit us.
That is the future that will come of us all.
So it goes with the world.

Angela Scott

Chaos

Keyonné McKnight

The Earth, in long-lasting agony, burnt to ashes.
The beautiful green earth going to a ferocious river of fire.
Such a beautiful sight to behold in fact,
So purely chaotic that you think it would be
The worst type of nightmare.

In a matter of hours, Earth was truly nothing.
Just a big ball of dirt and ashes.
There was no life to be seen.
No man, no beast, no plant.
Just eerily quiet with just the wind blowing occasionally,
Douching the last scuff of fire.

From a blank spot on the, now unrecognizable Earth,
The ground began to shake.

Shake.
Shake...until it finally cracked.
From deep inside Earth, two eggs shot up, as if possessed.
One was significantly smaller than the other.
The smaller one was a bright, neon blue.
Just staring at it too long was enough to blind the
Strongest man alive.
The large egg was a pastel green.
Those two eggs brought the color back to the Earth.

Even though they weren't much, they were consider the
First anything to bring life back to Earth.
From the day they first arrived all they did was
Blink, blink, blink.
Blink, unaware of the future that was to indulge them.
One day, the eggs showed signs of awakening.
The smaller sized egg stayed the same,
While the larger egg grew bigger and bigger.
When it finally stopped, it was the size of a human.

The smaller egg began to crack first.
It was deafening in the quiet environment.
The sound seemed to throw everything out of balance.
The little egg made a powerful sound that one would not
Think an egg would be capable of, coming from something
So small.

Roar, roar, roar the little egg cried out,
As if it wanted it's pain to be heard.
To be remember by all, even if there was no one there.
Maybe, just maybe,
The egg's cry would make someone arise out
From the clearing to seek out the anguishing cry.
After that terrible moment was through for the egg,
The shell just crumbled around it.
Out emerged a small living,breathing creature.

It was purple in color and smooth in texture.
The shape was a perfect square.
It had no mouth but it certainly had eyes.

Two ice blue eyes in fact that seem
To perfectly fit the creature's face.
Despite its bizarre colors, it was beautiful.
Especially to a planet which grew dark
And lonely without color.
The creature clearly had high forms
Of intelligence and perseverance
By the bright look in its eye.

The creature, after observing its surroundings,
Saw the second egg.
As if a mission was pre-recorded for it's
A voice began to talk in the creature's head.
"Greetings, I am be your inner voice. The purpose of my presence here is to guide you.
"This place is called Earth, but as you can see it has been demolished.
We were foretelling this event, but we weren't fully prepared.

"That's why we have gotten you,
The whole human race has gone extinct,
But we still want Earth to thrive,
Even if that means the end for humans.
Your job, along with the other egg,
Is to find a way to restore Earth,
And maybe start another race if we're lucky.

"To complete this task, we're going to give you
The first step of the process.

Then you have to figure out the rest on your own.
You are basically a computer chip, and all you have to do
Is fuse into the back of the neck of whatever comes out of
that egg.

"This is all of the information I can give you,
Please try your best, and good luck."
With this, the voice was cut off from the creature's head.

The little creature didn't know why he was chosen,
But he knew he had to restore Earth
Towards its original route of life.
He succeeded, and his story was to be told
For generations to come.
Of the savior of life,
When it was burnt to ashes.

7 On Change

2016

Everett Smith

Out with the old, in with the new.
I lost close friends, and I got some more, too.
I can't say it was easy, getting to this place.
A lot of time it was split, and I did it all at a pace.

Sometimes I still feel the pain of my past.
Since it's a new year, this breath will be it's last.
Now that's what I like to call
A blast from the past.

Black Hole

By Samiyah Fraiser

Spring is full of colors.
Pink , Purple, and Blue.
But that's until you take the mask off,
And realize it's true colors.

It was never those pretty colors.
It was crucial.
But welcomed into the environment.
My home.

It runs wild, like demons below us.
It gets you when you're asleep,
And when you're awake.
So sit back, and enjoy the ride.

As we go into Spring
When your life is at risk.
But look at the bright side,
It revolves around a black hole.

Forever Young

Kyeara Grate

Laughter.
Smiles.
Not a frown in sight.
Is this the break that we've been longing for?

I love the feeling.
Of not having a care in the world.
I wish to stay forever young.
Especially during break.

Its the perfect time for barbeques.
The best time for swimming pools.
A fabulous time for taking in the sun.
A great time to hang out with friends.

Company.
Joy.
Fun.
Is there a better way to describe this break?

Hoping My World Will Change

Jessica Bevins

Why does our world have to be this way?
I can't walk out my house without fearing death.
Wishing I had freedom to be independent and free.
Not having to worry about who might kidnap me.

Hoping that the world will change,
Knowing there will be no transformation.
I'm hoping and praying to see another day.
So as I go on to live the rest of my days.

I will forever be cognizant
Of the things I do and say,
Knowing there will be no transformation.
I'm just hoping that my world will change.

April Fools

Everett Smith

It's not April,
but I feel just like a fool.
People try to stunt,
But they're not even that cool.

At least I know my job,
and I still go to school.
They're always tryn' ta play me.
But I ain't a game of pool.

Okay, now let's get to the facts.
Some people are fake,
So they just know
How to act…

…for right now…

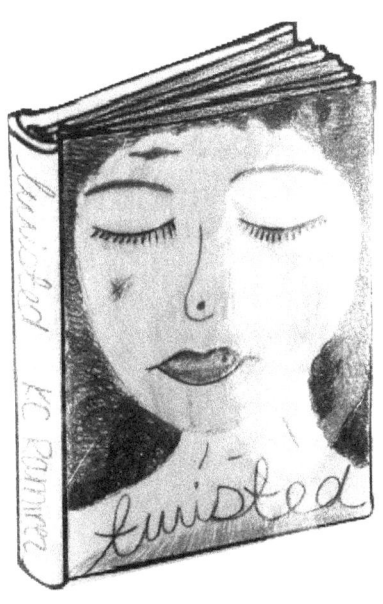

8 All About Love

Easy
Erica Stoker

You often have it easy, the two roads between the ratio
(Love : loss), (peace : life), Happiness : Stability
Often when you justify the obvious gap between the two,
And how often they do not mix.
You may be in love with him,
He had the dreamiest hazel green eyes,
But you have to find stability. You needed a paycheck?

I guess what I am saying is
I often wonder if the ones
Who are incrarcerated in their own inability
Choose the artistic route rather than the technical one.
I am tired of white picket fences,
And women coming home to men.

And men coming home to women
Whom they don't even truly love.
But they stuck together...
For the mortgage...
For the kids,
and for the paychecks (?)
But the ones who seemingly have nothing are always
The ones with heavy hearts.

I bet they all have beautiful minds,
I bet all students who go to
Art school instead of
Grad school, despite their
Father's disappointed glares,
Student loans out the wazoo,
But, she, I bet she had a
Beautiful
Mind.

I hope I have a beautiful mind,
But I may or may not be wrong
For I often think of
Killing myself
For no reason
At all.

If I

Syncere Washington

If I
Held you in my arms
If I
Cradled you to sleep
Would you say
That you still loved me?

If I
Cried myself to sleep
If I
Layed awake at night
Would you tell me
It's going to be alright?

Alfredo Flores

If I
Looked down when I walked
If I
Forgave how you lied
Would you still stay by my side?
If I...

Every Second
Kenya Williams

I once loved you.
You were my all.
But now I hate you.
Don't want you at all.

I wish you were gone.
Just leave.
My soul needs healing,
And you're the farthest from the cure.

I wanna hit you.
I wanna kick you.
I wanna kiss you.
I wanna hug you.

But I don't want you.
What's wrong with me?
Indecisiveness runs all through my body.
You are my poison.

A potion,
But no more.
My love has turned to pure hate,
And I'm dropping you.

You're no good for me,
If only, if only I knew

Just how to get over you.
But now your damage is done.

No more Hurting.

While you're sitting, having your fun,
I'm moving on to the next chapter of my life.

Every Second.

Angela Scott

Ride or Die

Zenaida Ingram

Ride or die, because she's mine.
She's my everything because, she's fam.
Not best friend, because there's no end.

She's family. I love you.

Is Life Worth It?

Rochelle Ortega

Everyone says life is beautiful.
Is it? Is it really?
Or is it the people in your life that make it beautiful?
I feel like some people make life easy,
Or some make it harder.

I can say that the people you care about the most,
Will be the ones also hurting you the most.
They will walk by you like y'all were nothing.
That person you would give your life for
Will be the one to stab you where it hurts the most…
The heart.

You can tell yourself that you never would think
That they would hurt you,
but one day they are going to say
They don't want to hurt you,
So they break your heart and they leave.
Now they don't talk to you
And it's so easy for them to act
Like you don't exist.

You thought you meant the world to them,
But you really didn't.
You were just a game to them.
Your feelings didn't mean anything to their soul…
My question is "Is life worth it?"

My Siren Song

Alyssa Kapinos

I sing with my delicate voice,
And the ears of men turn my direction.
They come here without a choice,
And I force them to give me their affection.

I draw the ship toward.
A path of jagged rocks,
And the ship could not afford
To head back to the nearby docks.

I dive inside upset water,
And make my way to the sailors,
To begin to slaughter,
Then drag their bodies to the bottoms of the deep.

Never trust the Siren's song,
Or the impression of beauty.
You would know you were wrong,
When you finally see your life flash before your eyes.

Shug
Shorace Guider

I used to love her,
Or at least I thought I did,
That is until she left me.

My heart became an abyss,
Where all emotions would just
Fall. The pit, bottomless.

My mind became an asylum,
Where it's contents were held in straight jackets
Never again to be free.

Why did she have to leave,
And take the only happiness I ever knew,
The only place I belonged
The only soul I felt was mine.

Now all that's left is anger,
And hurt. I was her through
Shaded eyes and broken dreams.

I was her between music notes
And staff lines.

Now I just sit quietly,
For my voice is gone.

What is the meaning of love?

Everett Smith

Love can be the form of a warm feeling.
Something that makes you float to the ceiling.
The love between two individuals is something so strong;
It must be original.

Love is not something that is meant to be broken,
And it can't be won with a coin or some token.
Love is not a simple game you can play,
Cause if someone gets hurt,
They'll take it the wrong way.

It could also
Be a gift.
From me,
To you.

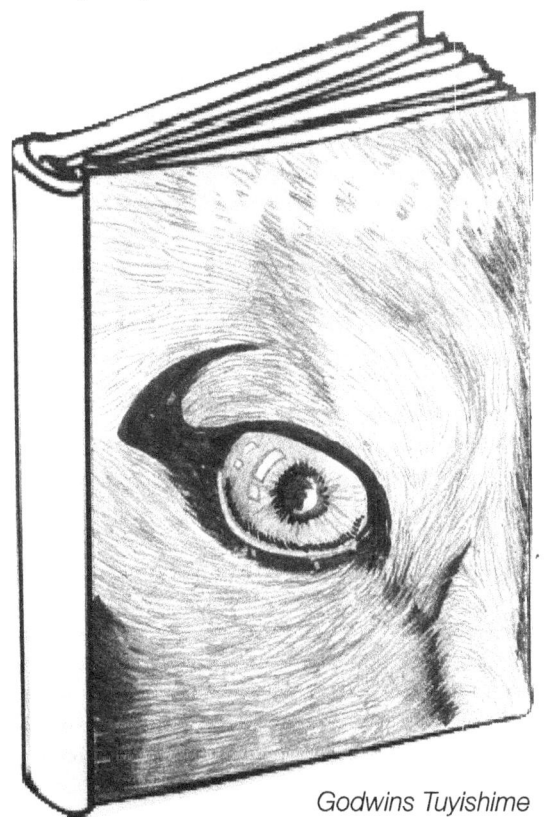

Godwins Tuyishime

What Shall I Do?

Kyeara Grate

You took the beat from my heart.
You snatched the rhythm of my soul.
I long for a way out of this place.
For this place is not my home.

Forgive me, I have sinned.
Repeats in my head.
I dread the times I've sinned,
And never forgave myself.

My infidelities.
Is all that seems to surround me.
I hate having to give it up,
But I must purge from the temptations.

I taste the blood.
I hear the fear.
I feel the energy of those who cry silently.
What shall I do?

Emmanuel Isaiah

Kyeara Grate

I miss you.
I love you.
You had my heart.
My Guardian Angel.

Baby Brother,
My first maternal.
I never saw you.
But we were always close.

I saw us together.
10 years and going.
I saw us growing old together.
I miss you so.

Emmanuel Isaiah,
Yahweh is with us.
You put your star in the sky.
I can't wait to see you.

Sweetness

Shorace Guider

The apartment doesn't smell the same,
The porch not as cozy,
The bikes await your return.
The pile of dirty dishes looks different;
There's no broken up sugar
Sprinkled on top.
Now who do I make eat over the sink
So crumbs won't get
On my kitchen floor.

I often compare you
To the "new you,"
But that just pisses me off even more
Because it's not you.

There's no honey bun wrapper
On the coffee table,
Between the remote
And the Diet Dr. Pepper bottle.

I don't laugh everyday
Like I did when your presence was guaranteed.

In the time you've been away
I've slept more
In my own bed,
And hurt more over the little things
You said weren't that serious.

You took those flip flops
That used to rest by the bathroom;
I don't trip anymore.
No one cooks, either. I don't worry
Where the scent of burnt popcorn or noodles is.
It's not there.

You took all of this away
When you left. "New you" tries to fill your shoes,
But she wears a ten, and would
Ruin your size eights. Overkill is what
I call it. Maybe one day we can
Pick up where we left off.

Maybe we can go to Krispy Kreme

Asylum

Kyeara Grate

I have been bondaged.
I have been broken.
This life has brought me no justice.
14 years in an asylum.

Progressing time,
Not a promising future.
This life has brought me pain.
14 years in an asylum.

Insanity slowly crawling up my sleeve.
I feel it reaching my mind.
My soul is falling apart.
My heart is stone cold.

My life,
My heartbeat,
My future,
All was left in the Asylum.

Don't Forget These Words

Kyeara Grate

The boys were talking struggle.
I call their bluff.
"Boy you blessed"
Haven't seen the heat of a bullet go through your chest.

If you bout it,
Lemme see where you stand.
We don't talk with guns,
Lemme see dem hands.

Ain't touch a tree in ya life.
Steady talking bout dope dealing is right.
Don't get yourself into no mess,
They may look like they engaged, but they ain't 'pressed.

Why you lying bout the game?
First rule you done broke.
If you was really bout it, you'd be nothing but a joke.

They got eyes and ears everywhere,
Oh you didn't know?
Just last night they been talking bout
Letting some people go.

Worried bout what's happenin in the streets,
Boy you better worry bout your life,
For God ain't promise us, but so much time.

Make your mama proud,
She knew you had it.
Walkin across that stage,
I know you almost grabbed it.

Instead, you can't resist,
They sorry dope dealer's life.
Smuggling on the streets,
You know it ain't right.

Mama sitting at the table cryin,
"Boy what'd you do",
The body that you caught last night,
Was the cold body of her little boo.

Don't worry though,
Cause as long as you makin dough,
You disregard yo mama feelings.
Feeling good on the outside,
But hell on the inside,
You don't know what to do.

You got the latest shoes,
clothes,
All the modern trends,
But did you help your mama meet ends?

Better learn to cherish what you got,

Cause nothing lasts forever.
Friends may fade away,
But God and family is forever.

'Member these words,
Cause I promise they'll come back to you,
Don't forget the lady,
Who helped you learn how to tie yo shoe.

Nyreon Alston

9 Troubles and Struggles

Hate

Yahira Gonzales

It's a word with a strong meaning.
A word that can crush millions if said by the wrong person.
Hate is a word with so much feeling.

A word that no one wants said to them.
Hate makes a difference in the sentence it's used in.
A meaning that not all will see.

Hate is a word. I never knew was going to hurt me.
A word that left me in tears for weeks.
Who would have known that one word could damage
Who I was?

I dread the day
Kyeara-Nyjae Grate

I can't believe it's over.
This break has come to a stop.
As sudden as a car
Being pulled over by a cop.

I took a trip to Philly,
But soon had to return.
I was very angry!
My face began to burn.

For when I return to school,
I shall dread the day.
I shall weep and hang low,
Like a dead flower in May.

I hope teachers feel the same way.
Maybe we can start a riot.
Tearing the schools apart,
Instead of staying quiet.

Finally One Has Come

Zamani Lyde

Oh, there goes another one, we think.
With every blast of a gun,
We forget about the past,
And what we have been able to surpass.

Another son has fallen.
But will we still rise together?
And strive together?
Although we've lost another part of us,
We are still able to unite to create one,
No matter the color of our skin.

Every voice comes from within.
So will you allow your voice to be heard?
While another part of us has died,
Together we can become one and fortify.

Free This Room

Shorace Guider

A little hope shines through the window of the
Dark room. At its center, a trapped spirit
Awaits its chance to taste air again. Even the rings
In the woods are moving toward the light. Is
Everything trying to escape? Splinters find hiding places

In invisible hands and knees, hoping it will
Be their way out. A better world can be seen
Through the holes in the floor. The cracks are wide
Enough to enslave a soul, but that would only slow
Down their journey. The room is as alone as its contents.

When will freedom show itself? The wood by the wall
Is closer to its destiny, for all the dreams coming
Through the window to find a resting place there.
The back of the room can only wish for joy.
Until then, waiting is the one and only option.

4:27 PM

Shorace Guider

I had worked an 8-4 shift that day.
Fortunately, Wendy's was just down the street.
I rode home with wonderful thoughts of
My mother making dinner,
My grandparents coming over,
The front yard.
All these things make me happy.

My father finished cutting the grass
As I pulled into the driveway.
He was so sweaty, but i hugged him anyway.
He said, "Yo momma's makin' dunna!"
I laughed to myself as I walked away.
That's why I think I feel so happy.

Everyone greeted me as I walked in the door.
It was so warm.
It was so memorable.
I looked at the clock on the stove.
4:25 P.M.

My father walked in a few seconds later,
Dripping sun rays onto the kitchen floor.
I was hot, lookin' at him.
The water turned on.
Daddy was washing his hands.
The water turned off.

I looked at the clock on the microwave.
4:27 P.M.

It was like my father was playing a huge drum set,
Hitting each wall with a piece of his body.
The noise was unbearable.
I was worried.
Until…
The bathroom door flew open.
My father fell to the floor with a sharp bang.
He was having a seizure.

His body quaked,
As if he was trying to break free.
My heart shuttered inside my frightened body.
I wanted to cry, but I had to be strong.
My father cried for me.

It was then I realized that you don't have to get wet to cry.
I felt like we were crying for the same reasons.
For the hurt to stop.
For the pain to be over.

I felt like time stood still.
I remember every breath.
Every moment.
It was at that point that I felt alone the most.
The silhouettes on the wall
Showed me my true loneliness.

When he finished, my heart stopped.
I looked at the clock on the vcr.
4:29 P.M.

I stood there in shock for a minute.
I was afraid to blink my eyes.
Everyone moved around me.
So fast.
So scared.

My father now laid there,
Motionless.
But breathing heavily.
His body was tired.
His brain was resting.

The clock kept ticking
As I walked to the kitchen
To clean the blood off the floor.

An ambulance was on its way.

We waited for help to arrive.
For a solution to present itself.
For hope to be restored
Back into our hearts.

My hands were shaking
As I moved the towel back and forth.

Godwins Tuyishime

The bleach made my eyes water,
But I wasn't crying.

It took them forever to get there.
I looked at my watch.
4:49 P.M.

Everyone was so still.
I remember the look in my mother's
Eyes that made me worry.

What was taking them so long?

When they finally got there,
My father was trying to get up off the floor.
He was immediately surrounded by cops.
Paramedics.
People he didn't know.

He was so afraid.
He started fighting them
As he cried and yelled out
My mother's name.

She tried to comfort him by yelling back
"Horace, I'm right here!"
The tears just ran down his face
And crashed to the floor
He was pushing back, so hard that
One of the paramedics had to sit on his legs

And the cop had to put handcuffs on him.
Two sets.

I think this made him angry,
And so he fought harder.
I stared at the bathroom clock.
5:16 P.M.

He screamed as he broke through one
Set of handcuffs.
His wrists were bleeding and blood
Still dripped from his mouth.
My eyes were filled with water.

If only they would have came
Sooner,
While he laid there, motionless.
But breathing heavily.

They finally got him to the ambulance.
He cried like a lost little boy.
He was so confused.

I stood there alone
As the ambulance drove away.
I turned on my phone at my phone.
5:39 P.M.

James Aiken

How Much A Dollar Cost?

Kory Singleton

inspired by Kendrick Lamar

Jamal walked to the store with intent on getting some change.
He was next in line which meant he was invisible.
His buggy had nothing, it wasn't even the slightest full.
The employee had some change in her hand,
But Jamal didn't look to play superhero,
So he walked out.
Marching to the beat of his band.
A policeman grabbed him, turned around and said,
"We got the burglar. Though nothing's in his hand."
Jamal knew he was in trouble, but thought
"Dang man, he's tan."

Jamal had been wrongly accused several times in the past.
This was nothing new to him, in fact he inspired some fans.
People watched the local news and watched Jamal get arrested.
Even though in the background, a new threat erected,
And a man in the back had a bag of money
Running away from the store, police thought,
"Dang man, it's funny."
"We caught the wrong man and he didn't even fight back!"
So Jamal sat in the cell, waiting for his bond.
He saw the local news and thought,
"How much that dollar cost?"

Robèrto sat outside, hoeing the ground,
His girlfriend had left him, his dog was in the pound.

Robèrto knew his life was going downhill.
Considered suicide, but
Didn't look to play superhero, so
He continued hoeing this other man's lawn.

The only way he could earn money cause he didn't know the law.
In the U.S., things are a lot different than anywhere else.
An apple hit him on the head, he snapped and launched himself
At the metal pole sticking out of the ground.

It had been sharpened over the years,
He noticed it's sharp, round shape
And tried to end it right there.
Starving, out of luck,
Roberto thought he felt the pole
Go through his heart.
He thought he was done and found a way out.

But when he woke up,
He found himself in a hospital.
The owner of the land had come outside
To check one Robèrto.
When Robèrto jumped on the blade,
He was rushed to the hospital
Where the owner found out Robèrto couldn't pay for insurance,
So he took care of it himself.
Off his salary, Robèrto couldn't even take care of himself.
It was a near-death, high-risk attempt to lose it all.
The owner spoke to Robèrto and asked,
"How much that dollar cost?"

I Won A Battle

Everett Smith

I won a battle, then lost another.
The only person I trust is my mother.

Most of the time, I forget the others.
Then I come back, and we greet each other.

We still smile, but it might be fake.
Our love Is colder than an Oreo milkshake.

This right here came straight from my heart.
Keep pushing me. We'll just fall apart.

Lost

Amiyah Wright

Walking in the middle of nowhere,
Not knowing what direction to take.
I'll call you back, I swear.
I just can't find a signal anywhere.

Walking in the dusty mist
Thinking about everyone I miss,
I have not eaten in weeks.
I'm feeling nice and weak.

My heart is broken,
Tears rolling down my face.
I'm filled with different emotions.
I can't wait to get home to have your embrace.

I'm hungry and I'm ready to flee.
I wanna be home. That's where I'm suppose to be.
I miss eating your homemade sweet peas.
When I arrive back home, I will be full of glee.

I'm sweating my heart out,
Dragging my two feet behind me.
Please don't give up on me, never have a doubt.
I used to be courageous, now I'm a nobody.

Walking to my deathbed,
But I'm not ready to say goodbye
I wanna be with you instead
When I get home, just be ready.

Never Will I Fold

Jasmain Jenkins

You may talk behind my back.
You may take my money.
You may take my loved ones.

You may rip my heart while it's still beating.
You may take my food while I'm still eating.
You may take my band-aid while I'm bleeding...
But never will I fold!

You may take my mom and capture my soul!
You may take my father and proclaim he's gold.

You may
Take my shoes.
You may
Take my house.
You can
Take my clothes.
But never my mouth!

You may take the Sun and you may take the Moon.
You may take the flower, but it will still bloom.

You may take my mom and capture my soul.
You may take my father
And proclaim he is gold, but...
NEVER WILL I FOLD!

New Life

Zamani Lyde

"Long ways up ahead!"
He yells, he says, he warns.
I grab my baggage and get up to leave the train.
Wherever I am is where I shall be, is where I should be.
My feet, heavy as if I've never walked with them before.
I stumble once more, unclear of why.

This place is different, I've never been here before,
I've dreamed of being here, living here.
This place now seems to be very familiar,
Familiar to my plans, hopes, me…
I look out at this new place.

As I look out I see myself
Screaming, crying, scared.
I run to her, look at her.
It's life.
I thought I fortified myself.
Only then did I enliven myself.

It's Life .
"Long ways ahead," I hear
I see a long road that's not paved
It's Life; But I am Strong.

The 4,000th Joke

Shorace Guider

I can't believe we're still laughing. I love this feeling,
Where I feel the blood slip through my arteries and veins,
Sliding through the capillaries, and bringing bliss to the
Most remote outposts of my body, delivering all the rich
Chemicals my cells crave, and ending with the most
Awesomely awful pain in my stomach. Stop, I can't
Breathe.

As tears rain from my eyes, I look at you and wish I could
Stop, but it's pointless. I'm drowning in laughter. You threw
That serious question at me like a life saver,
But it flew over my
Head, and is still floating somewhere around us. My chair is
No longer necessary for now I am rolling on the floor. Loud
Roars pour from my mouth as hahas turn to hehes,
Turn to giggles,
To chuckles, to dying.

I haven't felt this before, not in my whole 23 years
In this career
Of life. As the death of this time comes closer and closer,
A silence overcomes me. I've exhausted the possibility
Of language, and now all that can be heard
Is a puttering sound.

My mouth is open
And fun just keeps squeezing out.
I don't ever want to lose this.

But the moment passes, and we sigh
And make comments like
"Why you stupid?" and
"That's somethin' crazy people say,"
As the laughter continues to echo in our ears.
You know you still hear it.
And to think, all of this stemmed from one question:

Why do they put croutons in a stay fresh bag
when it's stale bread?

Angela Scott

Brianna Ramirez Tanner

10 Politics, As Usual

Gays Are Cool

Ta'Leigha Gibbs

Gays are cool.
Being gay is normal.
Being gay isn't disgusting.
I find these people wiser
Because they aren't afraid to show who they love.
Bullying someone
Because they are gay is not cool.
Does it matter if I am gay, or your best friend,
Or your neighbor?
That's right, it wouldn't matter.
If someone thinks being gay is wrong, they are being haters.
Don't judge people.
Gays are cool!

Donald Trump
Arianna Pinckney

Some people support him,
Some people hate him,
Some people understand him,
And some people are just like him.

Donald Trump, he has no heart.
He doesn't care about others.
He wants to stop immigrants from coming over the border,
But he doesn't understand
That some people are just trying to protect themselves
And others.

No...
All he sees are the jobs and homes that Americans won't have.

When Donald Trump sees somebody
That is not white, he sees negativity,
But that's no way to go through life.
Some people might not agree with what I'm saying,
But that's because they can't take the truth.

All this talk about Donald Trump making America better,
It's not the truth.
If Donald Trump becomes president,
He will make things worse.
All of his supporters will then see what he is all about...
Lies.

Donald Trump, a racist.
But his wife is from Sevnica, Slovenia,
And 24 years younger than him.
In my opinion,
Donald Trump is a mean,
Vain,
And cruel old man.

Donald Trump, A Leader?

Avni Scott

Donald Trump.
Why would anyone want him as a leader?
He will ruin you.
He'll bring back slavery.
He is a horrible person.
Just because he is rich
Does not make him nice.
Or smart.
Or a good person.
Please don't vote for him,
He will bring the worst in the world,
You have been through or heard about.
Donald Trump, a leader?

Memories
Daniel Hernandez

I was in a restaurant with my parents,
Eating my cookies with cinnamon,
When suddenly this lady approached us
And called us "illegal immigrants."

She was ignorant.
She said we weren't citizens.

At first, I couldn't comprehend.
Then, I couldn't understand.
But my mother started sobbing.
I was like, "Oh man."

We left the place immediately.
Nowadays we don't go there.
Once we got in the car,
That's when my father went berserk.

At the end of the day, we wondered, "why?"
Because, in society,
Immigrants always seem to be the bad guy.

Her words killed us that day
It kinda felt like a drive by.

Takasha Hagler

11 From The Mouths Of Babes

These are opinion pieces written by students who had very strong feelings about current events. They in no way reflect the opinions or posiitons of the Charleston County School District, Jerry Zucker Middle School of Science, or any member of The Zuckerbook Project's staff, and in particular their CEO, who chooses to stay out of all of this. Any and all correspondence should be directed to erik_hilden@charleston.k12.sc.us and will be given a good read and all due consideration. Thank you for your participation.

On Gun Control

Godwins Tuyishime

A friend of mine believes in this phrase, "Guns don't kill people, people kill people." Honestly, this is somewhat true, but like Donald Trump, this is the stupidest thing I've ever heard.

Guns give people a sense of not safety but power, dominance, superiority, etc. How do you think Superman would feel, if he had been raised differently, that his power would have gone to his head and, "Bam!" an empire is created. Kevin Ngo stated that President Obama has proposed a plan to have thorough background checks on those who purchased guns, and prohibit the purchase of armor piercing bullets, along with magazines with a capacity larger than ten bullets. This isn't a bad idea, until you realize the human race is quite intelligent; one bullet is enough to kill someone; the presence of a gun itself, unloaded, is enough to rob a store; even acting like you have a gun works.

    The Emanuel Nine would have been prevented if guns were harder to possess. Making guns nearly impossible to get would discourage people from trying and people that know the law would have peace of mind knowing shootings not done by policemen will be rare. As a matter of fact, rubber bullets don't kill anyone, they just hurt; I don't know why politicians haven't thought of that yet. I shall press no longer, I rest my case; guns don't have many pros, so if we really are smart, they should be in the wind soon.

Gun Control

Kenny Coronel

Over the last couple of years, many innocent people have died due to a bullet shot from a gun. In 2012, twenty children and six adults were fatally shot. Last year, nine adults were shot and killed, right here in Charleston. More than 100,000 people die each year in America from a gun.

I think that America should have stricter gun laws. I think a higher age limit should be set to purchase a gun. I also think that the person purchasing the gun should not have previous crimes committed and/or any mental health issues. This could potentially stop a lot of gun violence in America. This will eventually save a person's life.

I do understand why people would need a gun. Either way, it could end a life in a second if you decide to pull the trigger. There are of course other ways to defend yourself. A gun is optional, but not necessary. Just keep in mind that a gun is dangerous. It is not a toy, nor an accessory. It is a thing that could kill people. So do I agree that the guns laws should be stricter. Of course I do. Something needs to happen before it's too late.

On Gun Control

Tristan Fryer

Gun control laws limit the guns that the law abiding citizens can have to protect themselves against the criminals that have the guns, and courts will commonly reduce the charges in plea bargains. Newly passed gun laws want to delve into background checks on any gun purchases and want dealers to have licenses to sell.

After the shooting at Umpqua Community College in Oregon, Obama stated in a speech, "We collectively are answerable to those families who lose their loved ones because of our inaction." This statement is inaccurate on many accounts.

Many states are making gun laws on "law abiding citizens" to own, carry, and use guns. All of this does not make it easier for criminals to get guns, these laws are making it easier for citizens to use guns, so as to protect themselves from the criminals that want to hurt and kill them with their guns.

Having laws that aren't upheld in court is useless. When a man is tried in court, sometimes the lawyer will drop the smaller charges, like the misuse of guns, and possession of guns. They go after the larger stuff, like when a drug dealer is found with drugs and weapons. Yes it is a big deal, but why drop the laws that could be used?

When this happens, the sentence of the criminal is slightly shortened by a year or month, sometimes only by days. But with the longer time, people would not be dying from these criminals repeat offenses. They could be home right now, eating or having fun with their families, but instead they are six feet under their wives, girlfriends, husbands, boyfriends, daughters, sons, mothers, or fathers.

In answer to the president, I believe that we are doing plenty to protect ourselves and others. Gun laws shouldn't limit us in the use of guns. Instead, they should help us in protecting our country and the laws should be upheld in court.

No Changes to Gun Control Laws

Kory Singleton

In terms of gun control laws, there shouldn't be any changes, in my opinion. If anything, they should become strict. Some people say that they should go away, but that isn't going to help society in any way. Allowing more people to carry guns is basically going to slowly throw society down the drain.

Let's be honest, there are some people out there that may be safe with the guns because those people have self-control. But again, let's face it, the way that some people were raised and forced to grow up, many of them will be very trigger-happy, more so towards those people who are in love with videogames like Call of Duty or Battlefield. Some of them have trouble separating reality from virtual life and that just puts everyone in danger allowing these peoples to have or obtain these weapons a lot easier.

Eventually, out of fear, we'd break up into anarchy if everyone was allowed to obtain a gun because gun control laws eased up. It just doesn't make sense. Things have been just fine so far. There is no reason to change it.

Mass Shootings

Keyonne McKnight

For the last couple of years, incident with guns have been getting worse and worse. They get more horrific as the years go by. For example, the Sandy Hook shooting left twenty innocent children and six adults dead. This and several other incidents like this are reasons why gun control laws should be stricter.

Some may argue against this point by say that the citizens need to keep their guns to protect them against someone who might try to hurt them. This won't happen anymore or at least not that often if there are gun control laws. Even if this were to happen, there are other ways to defend yourself. By allowing gun control laws, this means that less of the mentally ill will be able to retrieve guns, stopping them from hurting themselves or others. The mentally ill will be able to get the help they need without anything having to escalate to drastic measures.
These reasons are why gun control laws should be stricter.

By making this little change, it could help the world become a much safer and more peaceful place to live in.

Police Brutality

Kyla Wright

Many African American males have been killed by cops, because of inappropriate police behavior. This has become one of the biggest problems in the United States. It seems that police officers are taking advantage of the job because they are the people who stop crime.

Just like in the Michael Brown case, when a young black male was shot and killed by a Ferguson police officer. Darren Wilson claimed that Brown was going to attack him, so he shot him 6 times. If he did not shoot at the officer, there was no point for him shoot the gun 6 times. If he was going to open fire he should have shot when Brown could not stand properly. Almost every week on the news we hear that an African American male who is unarmed, has been killed by a Caucasian officer. The majority of the time, the officer does not suffer any consequences that should be given, just because there is "not enough evidence."

Time after time, the officers claim that they were fearing for their life, while the unarmed man was running for HIS. While the country likes to worry about the business that goes on everywhere else in the world, we can barely control the problems that we have ourselves. People join together when a tragedy like this happens. You can not come together one day out of the year, you have to stick together all the time to put this problem to a stop.

Nosey Americans
Devonte Alston

It's quite odd to see a country that calls itself, "The Land of Opportunity," to be deemed by its own citizens as the "Nosey Americans." This country has spent so much time getting into everyone else's business, until they've recently established that they've had lot of their own problems to handle. One of which is a very old yet not yet solved one called police brutality.

Police brutality has really increased in the U.S. over the past thirty years from the beating of a cab driver due to a high speed chase, to a routine injury of a "criminal" in custody; this is usually from the cops who rest their knees on someone's neck when reading them their rights while almost paralyzing them. Last year, on December 11 of 2015, a man was shot by a cop in California after a rollover accident. The man had his head outside of the car, which gave the cop a feeling that he would inflict violence upon him. Because of that, the cop shot him.

In the end, the cop wasn't charged at all, but the man remained paralyzed for the rest of his life. Another incident involving police brutality would be during the Walter Scott shooting.

A former coast guard member by the name of Walter Scott was shot by a North Charleston cop whose name is Michael Slager. After being stopped by a cop for a broken taillight, he was confronted by the cop while contemplating what he should've done next. He decided to run, and because of that, the cop decided to pull out his gun, the first thing that a typical cop pulls out from instinct. The strange thing about this is the fact that another civilian decided to record it while it was happening.

That explains why most of our problems aren't solved already. After all, we are one of the most recognizable countries of the select few. Or at least, in the worst way possible.

Angela Scott

Police Brutality

Zamani Lyde

He was unarmed but he was dangerous! No, he wasn't dangerous, he was just an African American. For all the innocent black lives lost, what were their crimes? They have now placed body cameras on most officers. In the "first year after the cameras introduction, the use of force by officers declined 60%, and citizen complaints against police fell 88," says the Wall Street Journal.

Has this really helped? No, not at all. Lives are still being lost, even with these fancy new cameras. It all comes down to their morals, their integrity, and just how much they really care about other lives. Officers have began to lose respect and let their authority, let's just say, make them big headed. True, their use of force has declined by 60%, but there shouldn't have been room for force to go down in the first place. Were their complaints real, or just facts of wrongdoing?

Instead of spending money on good equipment for their police training camps, why don't they save some money and show the officer's ways to conduct themselves as human beings beneath the badge when situations with citizens go wrong? Especially for our black citizens. We must not forget Michael Brown, Walter Scott, and Sandra Bland. They share a few things in common - unarmed, black, and they're all dead. If their deaths don't stand as inappropriate police conduct, then what does?

They may be cops, they may wear a badge, but they are not exempt from the law which they're supposed to help uphold, demonstrating what is right and what is wrong.

Clinton and Trump

Ca'Shun Barr

Hillary Clinton and Donald Trump are the two current top leading candidates in their parties. Most Candidates tend to lie about their political promises, such as when George W. Bush said he was going to run-up to the 2003 Iraq invasion. They are both rather intelligent, yet very ignorant.

Donald Trump has said some rather stupid things yet the American public loves him. Why, I don't know nor understand. He has threatened to basically remove everyone from America except for white people, which is pretty racist, if you ask me. At the end of the day, they are both horrible choices. Donald Trump is a businessman, not a politician. He's only at the top because of his unorthodox approach to politics.

Hillary Clinton is a normal politician, who clearly follows the set rules of running for office. She is a very independent woman, who fights strongly for what she believes in and is not afraid to back down from a challenge. She would make smarter, more strategic choices for our economy, but her pride may overpower the choice of the right decision. Being the current global situation, I feel that might cause America to be here one day and gone the next.

The election for this year is awful. The choices may cause permanent damage upon America. So far no one can see the future, and it looks like obviously Donald Trump is the right choice. Even though America was built on immigration, those very same individuals are going to be kicked out. Donald Trump seems like that kid who runs for class president, makes campaign promises and can't follow up on them. If America lies in Donald Trump's hands, God have mercy.

Same-Sex Marriage

Ryanne Seabrook

I disagree with people that say gay marriage isn't ok. Yes, of course in the bible it says that two men shall not lay together, but for the people who are against it, I just wanna say "when did you start obeying the bible.... Never, because the bible also says that you shouldn't judge one another."

I feel like we are humans and we make big mistakes at times. Everyone always has to open there mouths and say something negative to bring someone down. Everyone is always treating gays different, okay, they made what they are now society can live with it, like they are not human, like they are imbeciles or animals.

Gays are not so different if they can get married and have a family. It's sad that we live in a world where everyone judges.

I Don't Care, but Go Bernie

Chris McGill

Honestly, I'm not really interested in politics. I never have been. But at my age, that's all you hear around Presidential Election time. I've only really been hearing about four politicians: Ted Cruz, Hillary Clinton, Bernie Sanders, and of course Donald Trump.

My mind's already made up on Donald Trump. I very much dislike him and hopes he doesn't get elected. Honestly, I want him to just drop out and never try again. At first I was maybe going to root for him because I was familiar with his name. But after I first heard his comment about building a wall to block out illegal immigrants, he lost me. Some of my closest friends families are immigrants or not american. I'm not going to go out and say that their illegal and just isolate them from my life. But I think that they deserve a chance to live a happy life just like Americans. And who is Donald Trump to cut families' chances at a happy life?

So I am against Donald Trump and I guess I'll be rooting for Hillary Clinton or Bernie Sanders. But, most likely Bernie Sanders, because he wants to make college free for everyone by taxing financial transactions. Just with that one thing he want to do he has my vote for President. GO BERNIE!

About Terrorism and ISIS

Chris McGill

A lot of people say that the U.S. is not doing enough to stop the Islamic State of Iraq and Syria (ISIS). The terrorist group led by Abu Bakr al-Baghdadi, are as of right now the United States's main threat. They are the most dangerous group in the world and they have no mercy. They have done mass executions, tortures, and has been able to draw recruits from 90 different countries.

One of ISIS' most successful recruiting methods were the beheading videos. ISIS has recorded videos of them executing prisoners by beheading them. Potential recruits see these videos as evidence of ISIS power and control, along with the organization's willingness to be completely ruthless in fulfilling their duties as Muslims. Another method they use for recruiting is using the latest social media and production techniques, expanding their ability to reach out to a wide group of possible recruits.

Even though there hasn't been many ISIS related attacks in the United States, I predict that there will be a huge attack or maybe even a war. ISIS is quickly expanding and getting more dangerous everyday. Already, ISIS controls more land than many nations.

President Barack Obama says he has a strategy to fight ISIS that will succeed. His plan is to stop ISIS through airstrikes and using his alliance with local forces.

However, he says he is going to take it slow,

saying "We have the right strategy and we are going to see it through." His strategy doesn't really sit well with partners back in the White House, but I however agree with it. If we just try to attack ISIS it might start a war that nobody wants. So, maybe not at the moment the U.S. doesn't seem to be doing enough to fight this dangerous group, but I believe that soon when we get everything figured out this will all end in our favor.

Illegal Immigration
Daniel Hernandez

Illegal immigration has always been a big topic in the US. I remember in the 2008 elections between McCain and Obama, there was always that debate about immigration. I honestly think most of "illegal immigrants" I know are either hardworking and came into the US looking for a better life for them and for their children.

Sure, I can agree that some are gangbangers, but that doesn't mean that you classify all illegal immigrants as "rapists" and "drug dealers." I feel like immigrants have contributed to this country a whole lot. Like, for example, fruit picking. Without these so called "illegal immigrants," who would pick the fruit? No one, which is the sad truth. So I have to say that the US should give an opportunity to these immigrants, because they are tired and tired about the cartels, the drugs, the gangs and the violence that rules their country.

Illegal Immigrants

Kory Singleton

On the subject of illegal immigrants, the matter should really be handled differently based on where it's happening. Here in America, it's a subject that has become too common. Simply put, the U.S. Is slowly overflowing with illegal immigrants that came here for a "fresh start," or to escape what was back in their original country and I'm okay with that.

I understand that here in the U.S.A. you have a lot more freedom than you do in most places around the world combined and couple that with a "working" justice system and the U.S. seems like a perfect place to be. So I say let them be here. Not to seem a horrible person, but honestly, if they're going to be here illegally, this probably means that they will have to work somewhere in order to get the money to buy things, but they won't get as much as the average worker (for the simple fact that they're here illegally), and that saves money for the economy or something else.

I don't know what it's like to have to fight and crawl to get here, but if it's so bad for them in their home country, that they can't become "legal (whatever that means)" then you should still let them in. People want to live their life or give their children the best life imaginable.

If they are willing to sacrifice a little pay to make it happen, let them. But, at least, allow them in to have the opportunity.

Illegal Immigration
Tristan Fryer

I can understand the reasons that people immigrate to the U. S. illegally…better lives, more money. On the other hand, there is a way to properly enter the country. Part of the nation's problem is that most of the immigrants are entering the wrong way. So they are illegal, and they don't pay taxes and the taxes the rest of us pay are so they live with free health care and free food. While most of these families are immigrating illegally is because they are afraid of the drug dealers and the gangs, some come to America to mooch off of welfare. They come to live illegally in a country that doesn't want them, because the country is paying for them to have free health care and free food.

Now, while some come to America for good reasons, others than for the wrong reasons, such as the black-market and drug-trade. With the overwhelming numbers that flow into America every day, it will be almost impossible to calculate the amount of danger coming into America. With much anger and hate going to Donald Trump, I must agree that the fence we have now is a little sad. A wall will do better with keeping illegally crossing immigrants out.

Fabiola Pena

12 Really Short Stories

A Frozen Mistletoe

Julia Guo

I was shaken by the mistletoe.
Now, I'm waiting outside this cursed house.
He knows not of my intruding presence.
The soft snow falls in my dark, tousled hair.
I question knocking.
Inside the house, I hear the melody of a newborn relationship.
As my body freezes, I tell myself, "Lifeless. Emotionless. It's all the same. What matters most is who's to blame."
Merry Christmas.

Blueberry
Devonte Alston

"Hey ma, did you make that blueberry pie?" I asked.

"Yeah, she did." Bob interjected.

"Where is it?" I asked, with my mouth watering.

"Don't worry about it." He said, while laughing at me.

"Ha ha! You stupid dw-" His laughter was interrupted by a sharp candy cane that appeared in his leg.

"That's your favorite flavor right… blueberry?" I asked with condescension, laughing at his cry of pain.

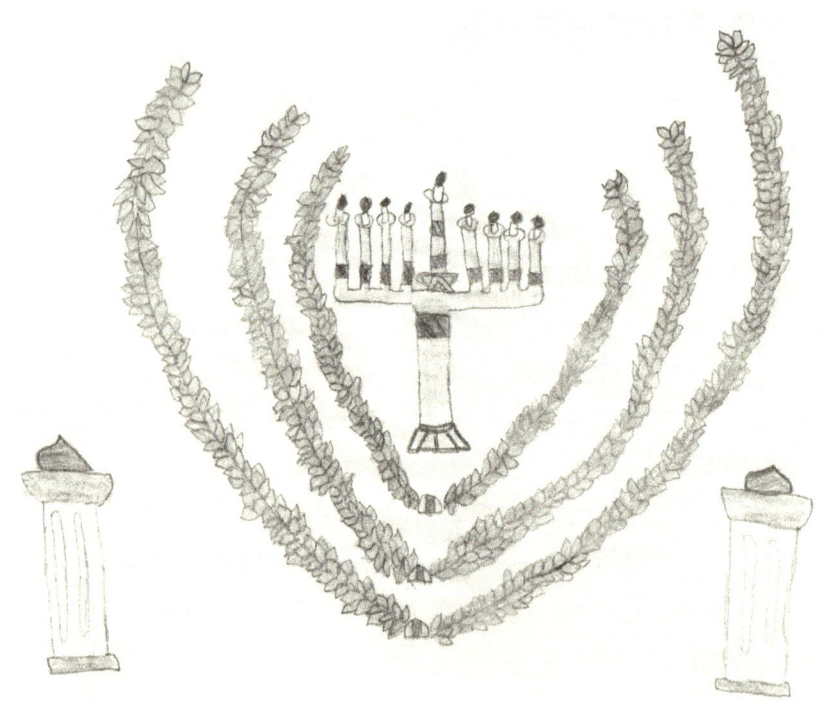

Jesus Verdugo

Jesus Verdugo

Bob won't be home anytime soon

Keyonne McKnight

Bob was in his car on Christmas Eve. He was driving to see his family for Christmas.

It was dark and he needed to stop. He soon arrived at a hotel.

"Room 13," the gruff manager says, crazily.

Bob opened the door ready to rest, when something unrecognizable attacks.

Screams echoed through the hotel along with the manager's insane laughter.

Bob won't be getting home anytime soon.

Dearly Beloved
Jack Sanders

"Dearly beloved, we are gathered here today-" The Pastor was rudely interrupted by an unnaturally shrill voice.

"No, No, No!" Uttered the irksome din.

"Please, be silent. We are here to celebrate-" The Pastor was once again imprudently interveined.

"It can not be!"

"If you cannot contain yourself, then please leave!" exclaimed the now irritated Pastor.

"I will not go, you cannot make me!" shouted the vexatious crescendo.

Whap!

"Pastor are you okay?"

"Yes, I just killed the fly that kept interrupting this joyous time. Do you…"

Jack Sanders

Frozen To Death
Godwins Tuyishime

"Why mommy?" I asked repeatedly, instead of working like she said.

"Honey, I know you think you can relax but a bad, bad thing is coming. So, Jimmy, keep working. Trust me."

But, unlike a good boy, I tricked my mother into letting me play.

Then, the next morning was hell. My mom went into hibernation, and I couldn't find the den. But if it weren't for Sven, I would have frozen to death.

Jack Sanders

I Had No Reply

Tristan Fryer

The youngest child walks into the room two hours after he was put to bed. The father cannot explain what happened. But the best I got was:

My child walked into the room and yelled, "I am here to tell you that Santa Claus will not be coming this year!"

When I asked why, the reply I got was quite disturbing.

"I found him on the roof; he was stuck in the chimney so I helped him down. I found a knife and cut him to size."

So I told him "Young man, Santa Claus is not real."

The reply I received was worse. "Then who was on the roof covered in red, yelling, "Ho-ho-ho?"

And to this, I had no reply. So the young one walked off, back to bed, not to remember what has transpired.

Jack Sanders

Nine Months To Go
Devonte Alston

I was sitting out on the porch with pesticide in my hand and my mother had just left the house.

"Well? What are you waiting for, a trophy?" she asked.

"Honestly, yeah." I answered.

"Just get it done." She ordered as I sat in front of millions of leaves, the only thing that I could see. I'm being told to cut them all down.

The Big Kahuna
Kyeara Grate

They ran to the shore.

"I can't wait to see the Big Kahuna" Max said.

"I wouldn't get too excited" Rosa responded. "The Big Kahuna is one scary wave"

Max couldn't understand his overprotective sister.

Big Kahuna had arrived.

They gathered their surfboards. Preparing for the wave, they drifted alongside it.

The wave broke.

"MAX!"

Sirens blared.

Spring Is Coming

Julia Guo

I'm waiting for my body to defreeze.
Slowly, my tips will thaw out.
"For now, I'll wait.", said Nature's creation.
My dead skin falls, brown and wrinkled.
The blizzard is my enemy.
There's no life in me when it's Winter.
The torture should be coming to an end.
I see green grass with no frosted flakes.
Just my luck.
"Timber!" called out a horrid man.

Why Is This Happening?

Kyla Wright

The spring break attitude was in the air.
"I didn't touch your belongings" she said.
Shana didn't believe her and said, "Don't do it again."
Complication everywhere. No one can get along for two days. Pitiful and immature and very annoying, knowing the fact that everyone could have been left alone.
Mamas were called and teachers were bothered.
Why is this happening?

Kenny Coronel

Blade Leaves
Devonte Alston

      "Woosh." Nature made that continuous sound at night.
      "Please tell me it's not raining," Said Godwins.
      Tap tap tap....
      "Go check and see," Said Trey.
      As Tyrell went to check, we felt as if he were checking for monsters in a horror film. For three years of watching out for raccoons, nothing had frightened me more than the leaves.
      "It's just leaves." Said Tyrell.

Shattered Joy

Devonte Alston

I spent so much time sleeping and lounging around. Lounging around at my grandma's house doing nothing. Nothing besides gathering up my thoughts. Thoughts of what may seem irrelevant to others.

After that, what has happened? Nothing!

Absolutely nothing!

I spent the past eight days, befuddled by myself. Saturated with uncertainty. Was I thankful for the little food that I ate? I hope.

Everyone around me was just so…happy.

I feel as if it was my job to shatter that joy. Obviously, it wasn't done correctly. Therefore, I did nothing for the holidays. Not yet.

I just need more time to forget about it.

Diana Acosta

Tahjai Spears

13 The Dark Side

It's 1:25 A.M.

Bianca Cedillo Perez

It's 1:25 A.M. right now.
I'm lying in bed right now.
I'm tucked in bed, with a hurting head,
And my arms are by my side right now.

It's 1:42 A.M. right now.
I'm sitting up in bed right now.
Eyes are bawling, Tears are falling,
And I'm trembling, please help me.

It's 2:09 A.M. right now.
I'm frozen, lying, in bed right now.
Face is Numb, Eyes are shut.
I think my time is over.

Chains

Amyah Wright

Locked in these rusty chains,
I'm being held against my will.
Why would you put me in such pain?
Please don't let this be a overkill.

You can't hold me back for long.
Don't be so cruel.
Can we just get along?
This is against the rules.

How long are you gonna let me suffer?
I can't take this no more.
This is such a discomfort.
LET ME GO! That's all I ask for.

What you are doing is not right.
I hope you will change your mind.
The chains feel worse then a snake bite.
You are such a evil mastermind.

How can you live this type of life?
Killing humankind and being content.
I rather be locked up in these dirty chains.
Then being horrible, like you.

You should be ashamed of yourself,
For hurting people and leading them to their deathbeds.

You should be removed!
You can't hold me back for long.

One day, you will regret doing this to me.
I will break away from these chains.
It's all because of your stupidity.
Because of you, I went through pain.
You should be ashamed!

Kenny Coronel

Living a Lie

Ca'Shun Barr

In awe, I sit back only to relax,
To take a look at this grand scale of a simulation called life.
Many times I had to double back twice,
Reincarnation although I don't deserve a second chance,
Life is life and I'll always want to succeed.

But maybe I need to secede,
To break away from the chains of the sex driven society,
Only to look in the eyes of our government
As they lie to me,
Forever I'll remember.

Forever I'll remember,
What you've done,
Traded against our society as a sinned son.
Blue bloods like both gangs,
Wrapped tight in bandanas with a silly name.

Trying to become a star,
Requesting nothing but fame,
Wanting dreams to last for an eternity,
As I shall not shed a tear,
Until the day I die.
Living a Lie.

Nightmare

Joel Orellana

I am the shiver cascading down your spine
While we are in complete darkness.
You and I clearly know
That you are not alone.

You thought you saw me in your closet,
And you did.
You thought I was under your bed,
And I was.

The darkness is my friend.
It is my realm.
You think you can run and hide.
But remember...you can't run forever.

You get tired,
I do not.
When you slow down,
I will catch you.

I will fill you with fear.
I'll fill you with despair.
I will snap you from your sweetest dreams.
I am...Nightmare.

James Aiken

Questions Not Yet Answered

Jalynn Henryhand

Why do leaves fall in the Fall?
Why do birds sing in the Spring?
Why is it such a bummer in the Summer?
Why is it a killer in the Winter?

Yet nobody knows.
We go far beyond stars and below dirt.
Searching for things unknown.
Unlocking secrets, mysteries.
Yet we never know what's in front of our eyes?

We gaze - we look - we peer - we observe,
Yet nobody knows.
Why did that atom burst creating galaxies
Far and unknown?
Why did Pangea break?
Why do we still let society belittle our minds?
Yet nobody knows.

Generations upon generations will investigate.
We will experiment.
Make of something left behind to be the unknown.
We shall rise.
We shall receive.
Yet nobody knows.

Nowhere to Hide

Kenya Williams

I tried to run,
But I was frozen.
Stuck in place,
Like my whole body was paralyzed.

I laughed,
Even when I wanted to cry.
Why though?
I get stuck questioning my emotions.

Do I really wanna be here?
In this unfamiliar place,
Where no one could hear me scream
If I regret this decision.

James Aiken

But where will I go
If I leave?
No one knows until they get there,
But then they won't be able to tell anyone.

That's why this whole thing
Is questionable.
Though no matter how many questions
You have,
You must not ask.
Nowhere to hide.

Pawn

Julia Guo

Empty, yet so full.
If I push, it will pull.
Out of madness, out of rage,
Out of loneliness, in a cage.

She will scream, but she will soar.
In the bright blue skies still on the floor.
Not a single touch,
Nor a gram of spirit.

It is locked in a prison of void,
Still believing such won't be destroyed.
Continuously shattering, continuously gone...
Of all the chess pieces, she is still the pawn.

Kenny Coronel

Nothing to hold

Jalynn Henryhand

I stare at my empty hands,
Cold palms and red finger tips,
Chewed nails-picked skin.

I have nothing.
I have nothing?

Lost in my own hate,
I let the one person I love slip out my grip.
Lost in the society,
Wild among the animals,
Still hunting for prey,
For I have already caught my catch,
Reaching my greedy hands out for more.

My hands fade through,
Numb-Lost.
I have nothing.
I lost everything?
Almost surreal.
I would bend down,
Beg on my knees for the relief of emptiness,
Just to get back what I once had.

I have nothing.

The Hurt Inside
Avni Scott

I was fine until I came here.
I always do something wrong.
Someone's always mad at me or something I do.
They say watch your back.

Or try to fight or hurt my feelings.
I don't know most of these people.
They hear rumors and don't like me.
Ugly, Stupid, nobody will ever like me.

Jasmain Jenkins

James Aiken

14 A Short Story

Dwell In Memory

Jalynn Henryhand

    The sound of a million buzzing bees. Oh, that is my Step-mother. My dumb blonde of a Step-mother. Brittney Wilson, or should I say, Brittney Banks. She is practically a stick, she hides her witch of a face under all that toxic makeup. She wears clothes that barely fit her body, showing off what little she has. I open my eyes almost as if a new driver is turning a corner at an intersection. Slow. All I can hear is the sound of my breathing. I make my way out of my king sized bed onto my royal blue carpet; I hate my life. I take my time getting ready for school. While doing so, I hear my step-mother rummaging through a sea of metals. I suppose she is trying to make food. I know that I'm not going to eat whatever she attempts to cook anyway; it's a waste of time...and health. I look in the mirror, staring at my wide hips, short legs, full chest, fluffy face and under my caramel tan skin. My same old, boring outfit. Perfectly ironed white button down collared shirt, blue plaid skirt, blue tie, blue blazer, school girl socks, and my timely old charcoal black shoes. Looking at my reflection in the mirror, I pick up my sack. I walk towards my door, take a deep breath and grab the handle. Then it all comes back.

"You will never be something!!"

"You are trash!!"

"I wish you were never born!!"

"You made him leave me!!"

"I hate you, I hate you, I hate you!!"

"You filthy piece of dirt…"

I pant as I slowly slide down the wall. I sob, remembering her. I can't believe she left, but then again, I could. I wanted to leave. Once again, all I can hear is my breathing. I hate my life. I stand, trying to gather myself once again. I can't let the pig think that I cry. I grab the door handle, quickly pulling it open; I don't want to have another vision. Hurrying down the steep stairway, pass the sitting area, towards the kitchen.

"Oh, hello sweetie, would you like some breakfast; I made-"

"Great I would love some!"

"Awesome, I made-"

"What makes you think I want anything you fix?" I answer harshly, unaware of my own tone.

"Look, I know we aren't on good terms, but I just wanted to do something nice," she said, almost as if she

Angela Scott

was a perfect angel.

"Well stop, I don't need your kindness, go back to where ever you came from."

"Wait, can we plea-"

I abruptly stop her by grabbing an apple and running out of the kitchen.

I will not lower myself to hold a conversation to a gold digger. I enter the corridor just as our butler is opening the extravagant front door, I hate life. I move to my white BMW 2015. I rush to put the key in the ignition; I feel like I'm running from a bad dream. My uncle cackles. My phone jumps up and down on the dashboard. Carl first inherited the business from my grandfather. To be honest was the perfect fit. Handsome, business man who leaves pregnant women when they're in need. He left us. Him leaving me with my abusive mother really did open my eyes. He was a player, jumping from club to club, women to women. He happen to stumble upon my very intoxicated mom, therefore starting my development. He left when I was a baby...a vulnerable, clueless baby. He dare had the nerve to come back five years later to look at the child he denied was his. He was never there, then my mom went insane. Breathe. Backing down the large driveway, I make my way to confinement; school. My phone jumps again, only it's a message. Father; I ignore it. I hate my life.

"You will never make it."

"I hate you, I wish you were never born."

"You took my life."

"Please, stop it mommy."

"That's not true!"

I gasp, swerving off the road, barely missing the car in front of me. Honk. Honk. Aw, screw you too. White light is all I see. Crash. Black. Honk. Honk. Weeoh. Weeoh. Ugh, my back. Blood is all I see.

Beep. beep. beep. Ugh, this pain in my head won't go away. I thought I was dead, but they

Angela Scott

can't possibly give me that satisfaction.

"Doctor, she's awake!"

I watch as I see the fairly young man walk in with a clipboard and wearing a white over coat. I can't help but wonder who let him become a doctor dealing with real, live humans, but we all make mistakes. I hate my life.

"Ah, well it's glad to see you awake after that horrid crash you had missy." the doctors says smiling a little too much for my comfort.

I try to talk but my voice is just too parched. I can see that the nurse recognizes my struggle and walks out for a drink. I almost want to yell and say stop I don't need nothing to drink because I want to die of parchness, if that's even a thing. Sadly I don't, with her coming to my side with a foam cup of what I presume as tap water. Ugh, filthy. Who drinks this stuff? It's so unclean. I drink it anyway, giving hope that I will be able to tell them I'm still alive and functional at this point, sadly. Though I assume they have already figured that out themselves.

"I'm fine," I say, my voice hoarse.

"Well, your parents are outside-"

"They're not my parents," I say quickly. They aren't my parents, they never act like it. I'd be crazy if I let a stranger call that blonde troll my mother. She will never be my mother, ever.

"I can't believe you call yourself a daughter, no daughter of mine I say."

"You will continue to torture my life."

"You were never suppose to be born."

"I HATE YOU!"

I shake my head furiously. She is gone, but my pain

is not.

"Umm ok, well they- want to see you, if they may," he looks at me as if i'm suppose to give the okay.

"I guess they can come in."

I wait literally four seconds before big mouth comes in.

"Ooh darling, I was so worried," she comes around lightly touching my face.

"DON'T TOUCH ME!"

She looks at me wide eyes, as if I'm the devil herself.

"And I'm not your darling either, god you make me hurl." I say looking her dead straight in the eye right before I actually feel like hurling.

"Look, I understand you're hurting but that's no way to speak to your mo-," my father attempts to say.

"What father, you mean mother; is that what you're trying to say?"

"I know she may not be your...mother but she is something and you need to respect that."

The nerve of him. Respect. I almost laugh. The nerve of him to talk to me about respect yet you so hold the key to my life.

"Honey we have to go, remember," she stares at him oh so lovingly.

"Right, Astrid you will be in here for about three days, I need you to behave so that I can prepare your court hearing," my father states.

"Hearing, hearing for what?"

"From the crash, we need to sort out this ordeal,

and you will behave and stay put in this hospital, understand!"

"Oh I understand, father."

"Don't you care at all?"

"I care as much as you cared about mom; about me." I stare at him dead in the eye, showing him the seriousness I hold.

"Let's go Brittney," my father states to the troll and all the while still looking at me.

I can see the nurse sending me an apologetic look. She slowly walks up to be with bottles in her hand.

"Here are-."

"Get out."

Her face quickly turns to fear as she immediately sets the orange bottles down and shuffles out the room.

Three days in this hell space. I wonder if I'm even capable of seeing the outside world. I see my father has done the decency of gathering my stuff out of the hospital dressers. I finally get to leave. I make my way to pull out the IVs in my arm but the doctor quickly stops me saying that he will do it so I won't injure myself. He pulls out the needle, but his hand still lingers on my arm a little longer than I would have appreciated. I twist my arm out his hold and look at him crazy. Once Carl and Dr. Theo hash out my paperwork, I bolt out the room, running down the halls. I hate my life. I make out the front and the very elegant auntie Essie is in her Audi A4 2009.

"Come on and hop in. I know you don't wanna ride with your father," my angelic auntie states. I happily jump in the car and Auntie Essie speeds off, my guardian angel.

She has always been my favorite. She is my real mother, she treats me as her own, she treats me equal, she treats me-me.

"How did you know I was in the hospital?" I speak for the first time.

"Well you know your father doesn't tell anything, but I'm always watching my darling."

I always believe that. I truly do believe that my auntie has powers.

"Honey, I would love to spend the whole day with you throwing darts at your father's head, but I have an extremely important meeting so I'm taking you home, I just wanted to give you a ride and check up on you; is that alright?"

"Yes, I will be fine; thank you auntie," I state, slowly closing my eyes and letting in the lethal breeze.

I make it home safely, and watching my guardian angel back out the driveway blowing me a goodbye kiss. She is such a tease. I walk into my home and walk all the way to my room. Of course the happy couple walks in four hours later, and Brittney calls me down for some kind of conference. I walk behind her sending her hateful glares at the back of her head. Breathe. I sit at the table and look at my father. Show no emotion Astrid. Breathe.

"We have decided to send you to Croons Willow Academy, no argument; it's to help you and your behavior, Astrid," Carl states. I look at Brittney.

"How long will I be there?"

"For as long as needed." Brittney answers with a loving gaze towards my father. Looking for approval I see.

"Okay."

I may not be struggling now, but anything to get away from these people.

"When do I leave?" I ask.

"Today." Carl states with a straight face.

"He will never want you!"

"He will send you away someday, I swear!"

"You fat pig, get up and go clean that mess…"
I shake my head, while regaining my focus. I turn away and run all the way to my room. Slamming my door and slumping against the wall. Don't cry, no more tears. They don't deserve it. She doesn't deserve it. Big men barge in my room dressed in all white.

"Hey, what do you thi- HEY, ahhhh," I scream as one of them lifts me up over their shoulders and carries me through the maze of the elegant house. I see pictures hang upon the wall as we pass by. Everything is so loud, I barely hear my screaming for release. The last picture I see is Elizabeth Heart Banks, my mother.

I'm trapped in this room for hours. No one has bothered to walk in this room since I came here. One window with silk blue curtains, one walk-in closet, bathroom on the left, and king sized bed in the middle with soft silk sheets covering the interior. Nothing else, no dresser, TV or even another chair or bench. Just me, sitting here on the foot of the cloud. I finally see a different man walk in with a tray of hot food. He thrust it out to me but when he sees I don't take it, he just sets in on the bed and walks back out the room. Slam. I look at the food; mash potatoes, beef and gravy with corn on the side. I grab the tray and eat slowly savoring of what might be my last meal. Then I see a different man walk in with another man and women on either side of him. He had dark green eyes and his skins was flawless he truly look like an Adonis. Standing at 6'1, he was definitely two heads taller than me.

"Well hello there, I hear you're our newest member so let me welcome you to Croons Willow Academy." the first man says as he holds out his hand. I turn from his face and look at his hand for quite a while. Does he expect me to shake that?

"Well where are my manners, my name in Jacob Anthony Willow; here are my assistants." he says as he points to himself and the two behind him.

"What is your name?" the lady behind him ask. I wait a while before I finally decide to tell my name.

"Astrid...Astrid Halo Banks."

"Astrid, what a beautiful name," Jacob says staring in my eyes. I keep a straight face. He is not ugly, he is very handsome, just creepy, very creepy. I turn my head away.

Angela Scott

"Could you please get her a uniform. I hope your alright because you're starting today."

"Starting what?"

He never answered my question, he just left. The other had already left soon returning back with a light blue uniform. It looked like a nurse scrub, I would only know because my mother used to be a nurse.

"Astrid, I'm home; did you do your homework"

"Astrid?"

Twenty minutes later the same lady that was with Jacob came in and look at me.

"Why haven't you changed into your uniform?" she asked staring at me.

I didn't answer. I don't have to. She means nothing to me, and I'm leaving this place the first chance I get. I'm not suppose to be here, my father sent me here. He sent me away, mother was right. He was never there and he never will be.

"Look, you need to change into your uniform, Mr. Willow will be here soon to show you your job."

I stood and started to pull off my old clothes, eyes full of tears and betrayal.

"The bathroom is on the left." she said finally walking out the room. Taking a shower I thought of all the things I have been through in the last few days. I bet Brittney put him up to it. I wash my short jet black hair with the pomegranate splash scent, in the curvy bottle. I quickly dry off, and reach for the handle.

"COME OUT RIGHT NOW, ASTRID!!!"

"You can't hide forever!!"

I gasp immediately pulling my hand back. Maybe I am afraid I will see my mother on the other side. I can't take the abuse again. It still left dark scars upon my body. I look right on my shoulder to see my very first scars from the she-devil herself. Only in my eyes it would look as a fresh cut than to the average. I turn to stare at the handle, once again reaching and succeeding to pull the wall open. I walk out noticing a cool breeze, shivering I look up from my feet to see Jacob himself.

"Aaaah!" I look at him wide eyes. He stares at me as if he has no problem in the world, like he belongs here.

"What are you doing in here!" I ask bewildered. He gazes at the bed, brushing his finger along the dark wood. I am yet still bewildered at why this man decided to interrupt my private time.

"GET OUT!"

He looks at me once again.

"Meet me outside the door, and don't ever speak to me like that again." He growls giving me an intense stare. I hurry to put on the garment scared he could walk in again. I open the door to be met with Jacob Anthony Willow himself.

"Come." He says, turning around heading the opposite way. I carefully follow him along, taking in my surrounding for future purposes. We walk almost a silent decade before we come to a huge door. I could almost feel the power radiating from the inside. Jacob opens the door and pushes his hand in a gentlemanly way. I hesittate before finally taking a step and entering the large office. It smells like him, Jacob. I stand behind the two large swivel chairs,

I hear a click. Turning around I see Jacob take his hand off the handle and walk behind his desk. He sits down in his leather chair behind his mahogany desk and looks me right in the eyes. Staring, trying to search for something.

"You may sit," he says. I sit down, and looks around the very dark office, with a bookshelf filled with books on my left.

"Do you read?" he ask me.

"I used to," I admit.

"Well maybe when you're on break you can read one of my collections," he says.

I just nod my head in agreement and turn to him once again, looking at his sharp, chiseled jaw.

"I have decided you will be my personal assistant," he says.

"I thought you have those two people."

"Yes, but they work around the castle, I need someone here, close to me," he says looking at me up and down intently.

"You barely know me." I counter.

"Yes, but I need an assistant and something tells me that you would be a great one." he looks into my hazel eyes.

"When do I start?" I say, and he smirks.

"Right now, you will be sorting my paperwork; ABC order." he pulls out a huge stack full of papers. Then he shows me a huge black cabinet.

"I will be back to take you to lunch," he says, looking at me up and down once again leaving with a smirk on his god-like face.

I worked for two hours until Jacob came back to get me for lunch. I even sat with him, I could see the other workers looking at me crazy for sitting with him. He sent an escort to help me to my room where I'm currently bedding. It's so soft, much finer than the one I had at- I can't think of that right now. I have to escape. Luckily, I snuck a fork from dinner when Jacob wasn't looking. I get up and shower. Breathe.

"You're ugly!"

"No one will love you!"

"Look at you, pig!"

I collapse on the bathroom floor. Breathe. Breathe. Breathe. I stand up and get ready for the day. Once my neatly ironed and folded uniform is on I step out the room. Push my shirt down one more time to start my journey to Jacob's office. On my way I come across the kitchen, quickly sneaking in after checking my surroundings for guards. I look around until I come across a small pocket knife and hid it down my pants. I check my surrounds again and sneak out, immediately heading back to my chambers. I hide my possible chance of freedom along with my sense and head back to Jacob's office. When I get there I knock on the heavy wood.

"You may enter," I hear a voice coming from inside. I enter to see Jacob at his desk. He swipes off his reading glasses and looks at me intently. I turn my head away, afraid of showing emotion.

"Thank you for yesterday, you did a wonderful job." I look at him again.

"You don't smile a lot do you?" he asks.

Angela Scott

"I have nothing to smile for," I say, keeping a straight face.

He stands up slowly walking around his desk toward me. I stand up backing away from him. His well manicured hands sweep across my cheek as I close my eyes and scrunch up my nose. I feel his other hand grip my waist as I struggle to get out of his hold. He ends up grabbing my jaw, growling at me in frustration. Knock. Knock. Knock.

"Sorry to bother sir, but we have a situation down in quarter B," said a simple man behind the secured door. I look at Jacob, into his eyes, as he stares in mine.

"Okay, I'm on my way." Satisfied with the answer, the footsteps quickly leave the halls.

"I'll be back, and you better be here," he says, me knowing he is not kidding. I nod my head in reassurance. He walks out the room not looking back. Breathe. Breathe. Breathe.

"Whip. Whip. Whip."

"Mommie!!!"

"SHUT UP!!"

"AAhhh!!"

I can still smell the thick crimson liquid. My whole body shakes. I have to get out of here. I turn, rampaging through the dark wood drawers. I see a map outline of the entire estate, quickly grab it and hide it safely. I crack open the heavy doors looking down the hallways. No one is here. I open it all the way, speed walking towards the room, staying alert for anyone associated with Jacob. I make it to the room, quickly grabbing all the items gathered over the two days. I leave the room, swiveling myself through the maze of the ancient castle. I make my way to the last hall I see a guard.

"Hey, there she is!" he says looking down the hallway next to him.

I see Jacob has realized I'm gone. That means I can't mess this up. This is my first and last chance to escape. I run the opposite way, bumping into another guard. I see him fall to his knees, crimson trickling from the gash in his neck. I gasp.

"You weren't there!"

"She beat me, She tortured me, She abused me!"

"You were never there!"

Backing away from the scene, I continue running down the halls. Everything in slow motion, all I can comprehend is my breathing. Breathe. Breathe. Breathe. I make it through the back door heading to the indoor garden. No. I look behind me to see five guards. I stand no chance.

I run all the way to the glass wall, looking down I see a pool. Breathe. Crash. Pulling my arms up to my face. Ouch. Glass pierces my skin, but all I can feel is freedom. Splash. Perfect landing in the pool. I swim to the end, lifting myself up. I run to the woods. My short jet black hair blowing through the wind. Duck, jump, run, duck, jump, run, I continue my escape at no end. I see a road ahead, using the last of my energy to run to dark cement. I walk along the road, hoping for upcoming civilization.

"Ouch!" I cry out.
My cuts and scrapes are getting worst, I need to get clean.

"Uhhh," I sigh looking at the pieces of bloody glass in my skin.

The fact I may never see my family again sets in. My auntie Essie, my mother, my father they're all gone. I have to start fresh. I remember that day my mother and I had to start over.

"Mommie, mommie, mommie, I love you!" I say smiling at my beautiful red head mom.

She holds her perfectly tan skin, and long legs as smoke comes from her red puckered lips.

"I love you too, doll," my mother says looking at me with a smile, then back at my father's red car back out the driveway.

I see Grudge Way show up. Maybe it's a bar? I walk up, smelling the poisonous liquid. I enter as some eyes turn to my attention. Then I realize I still have dried tears, dirt and blood upon my face. I speed walk my way to the ladies bathroom across the hut. Strong, sour leftover food that didn't settle infiltrate my sensitive nose. I cover my nose, keeping me from emptying my empty stomach. I see the sink and immediately make my way to it. Wetting the paper towel and wiping all the past off my face. I finally stop and look at my reflection in the mirror. Dried dirt, leaves, and glass shards left in my jet black hair; dirty and red stained light blue scrub. I look as a tear falls down my defeated face. I wipe it off, wash the dirt off my hands and exit the fowl bathroom. I sit at the bar for a while. A really pale lady sits a drink in front of me saying it's on the house. I push the wet glass away but after a while I realise that drink looks good in my situation. I take a sip as the liquid burns down my throat. It's time to go, it's midnight and their closing. I have no idea where to go or what to do but I still go outside. Breathe. Cough. I see the bikers' motorcycles lined up side by side as some of them start up and roll down the hill. I see the trees on the other side of the road and just stare for a minute. I shiver as the cold is finally getting to me. Someone grabs my arms and holds it down, while placing another hand over my mouth. I try to loosen the predator's grip, but their too strong.

"You're MINE!" I finally give up, shaken, I hear Jacob Anthony Willow's voice.

I remember the second time my father left us.

"I love you mommie." I say looking at my goddess of a mother.

"I love you too, doll." she says while holding my hand watching my father back down the driveway, leaving us forever.

I always told my mother that I loved her every time my father left. What really happened between my father and mother , that caused so much pain in my life. Maybe it's time to dwell in my memory.

Angela Scott

Nakleh Villasenor

Epilogue

Dedication is evident when desire and inclination converge. That sounds kind of profound, doesn't it? It is. It is what happens whenever a group of people put their minds together, become a team, and approach a task that seems insurmountable. This year, our staff, with yours truly doing what he can to a) offer guidance and resources and b) stay out of the way, have managed to publish two volumes of student writing and art in a single school year.

Great things have happened as a result of all of this hard work. First and foremost, the two volumes are the best we have had to offer yet. Students really stepped up to the plate and produced writing and art that shows the quality of these students, our faculty, and our school. This is awesome. They also produced more than we could use, which has given us the luxury of being more selective than we were in past issues. We have enough art to keep us busy for many issues in the future, which is also fantastic.

The Zuckerbook Project has also been able to support the school by donating to many DonorsChoose.org grants for our faculty and staff, supporting the basketball team by partially funding their banquet, the soccer team by helping them buy uniforms and soccer jackets, several teachers buy equipment for their classrooms, and a violin for our former stroings teacher, as well as several guitars for After School Guitar Club. We have also purchased two Apple iMacs with complete versions of Adobe Creative Suites 6 so that we can bring more of our production in house, rather than bother our friends at

Studiohawk with assembling the entire project. Now, we can bring edited images and art to them rather than sending them the pieces and occupying much of their time, which is donated to us out of their belief that what we are doing is beneficial to our students.

All of this is great, but there is so much more to do, and so much more to learn. We have come a long way, but we have a long way to go before our dreams of being a self-sufficient entity that teaches students trade skills in desktop publishing and business while remaining an elective class in writing and art can be realized. A lot of that, of course, is on me. I am fine with that.

We managed to hone our team down to eleven students in three teams. This was an important first step. We have had a measure of success in selling our books, which is also great. We have managed to hash out ideas about how to produce other products besides books…a boardgame based on Monopoly, for instance, and possibly a tee-shirt. We have our Square Store up and running, our website up and running, a presence on social media (Facebook, Twitter, Tumblr, Instagram, Snapchat, Pinterest, and Vine) that is slowly growing and interesting the Public Relations team in marketing through the social network channel. All of that is well and good, but we need to get to the next level.

This means selling enough of our books to cover our expenses, and not having to rely on fundraising efforts to fund our publishing and support our donations to the school. We need to figure out how to get attention from the local media, because they have ignored us almost completely, in spite of the great things we are doing for the Zucker Middle School community. We need to figure out the steps to this process so that it can happen a lot more quickly with a lot less error. So, processes must be created that work for everyone, and work well; protocols must be created and followed, so that everyone knows where everything is at all times; reasonable timelines must be discussed and followed, so that we are always on time and respecting deadlines; connections need to be made and maintained so we can appear in the public eye and remain there. In short, we need to become a real publishing house, publishing real books and bringing them to market, run out of a middle school classroom and operated by middle school students.

And not one of us, myself included, knows exactly how to go about these tasks. None of it is too much, but it all requires a degree of organization that is difficult to achieve in an uncredited elective class.

Nothing is impossible. Of this we are certain. We just have to change our approach. It is really that simple.

But how?

A massive reorganization of the class is in order for next year. We did many things successfully this year, but we can do a lot better. If we can manage to collect more than we need for this issue and be selective in what we choose to publish, then we can figure out how to get these books into book events, book stores, and libraries around the county. If we can set up and operate an online store, we can figure out how to streamline our shipping process. If we can use social media, then we can figure out how to use it as a targeted marketing strategy. Every single one of these entities exist within our community. We just need to access them, learn from them, and employ what we have learned.

We also need to take ourselves seriously. This issue is an attempt to do exactly that. The usual poetry is included…honest expressions of teen angst, heartbreak, creative thought and adventure. We have also included short stories and micro-ficiton pieces, which are entertaining and fun to read.

To bring things up a notch or two, we have included our first opinion chapter, addressing student concerns on politics and current events. Let me be the first to say that, though we are excited to present these pieces, they and the opinions they express are in no way intended to express the opinions or positions of The Zuckerbook Project, its staff, Zucker Middle School's faculty or administration, or the Charleston County School District. They are offered as a peek into the window of the teenage mind, what their concerns are, and how they feel about those things that adults discuss on a daily basis, or watch on the news. It is easy to forget that young adults and children have these things on their minds, as well, and easier to forget that their opinions are just as relevant as ours. I found them surprising, passionate, and fascinating, and I hope that you will, as well.

As we look to the future, we see the trails that are laid out before us. We know that few of these trails have arrows pointing to desired destinations, and that there is no roadmap for an endeavor such as ours. That's okay. We love the adventure. We love the mystery. And we look forward to moving The Zuckerbook Project into the arena of successful publishing, one volume at a time. Thank you so much for your support, and thank you so much for purchasing our book. We hope that it gives you a new way to see the students we take for granted almost every day, and to begin to view them as the intelligent, engaged, and skilled people that they are, and always have been. It has been a glorious ride, but that ride is far from over. We welcome you to ride along with us.

With grattitude, a tip of the hat, and a big ol' smile,

Erik J. Hilden
April 2nd, 2016

www.ingramcontent.com/pod-product-compliance
Lightning Source LLC
Chambersburg PA
CBHW020854090426
42736CB00008B/370